The Ultimate
Soul Music
Trivia Book

The Ultimate Soul Music Trivia Book

501 Questions and Answers
About Motown, Rhythm & Blues,
and More

Bobby Bennett
and
Sarah Smith

A Citadel Press Book
Published by Carol Publishing Group

A Citadel Press Book
Published by Carol Publishing Group
Citadel Press is a registered trademark of Carol Communications,
Inc.

Editorial, sales and distribution, rights and permissions inquiries
should be addressed to Carol Publishing Group, 120 Enterprise
Avenue, Secaucus, N.J. 07094.

In Canada: Canadian Manda Group, One Atlantic Avenue, Suite
105, Toronto, Ontario M6K 3E7

Carol Publishing Group books may be purchased in bulk at special
discounts for sales promotion, fund-raising, or educational purposes.
Special editions can be created to specifications. For details, contact
Special Sales Department, Carol Publishing Group, 120 Enterprise
Avenue, Secaucus, N.J. 07094.

Manufactured in the United States of America
10 9 8 7 6 5 4 3 2

Library of Congress Cataloging-in-Publication Data
Bennett, Bobby.
    The ultimate soul music trivia book : 501 questions and answers
about Motown, rhythm & blues, and more / Bobby Bennett and Sarah
Smith.
      p.   cm.
    "A Citadel Press Book."
    ISBN 0-8065-1923-1 (pb)
    1. Soul music—Miscellanea.   2. Rhythm and blues music—
Miscellanea.   I. Smith, Sarah, 1943–   .   II. Title.
ML3537.B46 1997
781.644—dc21   97-27572
                                                                       CIP
                                                                       MN

Acknowledgments

The authors express their gratitude to Flavia, Connie, Eric, Faith and E. J. Payne, Bob Manuel, Jay Johnson, Lou Hankins, Bessie Wash, Jimmy Smith, Jack Daniels (the man, not the whiskey), James Bearden, Esq., the Payne brothers, Ray, Gary, and Tony, the late Edith Edelin, Caira White, Tynea Handy, DacRon Hobbs Jr., Oleta Finch, Marjorie Stewart, Marie Kelley, Cindi Grant Mulzac, and Carolyn Smith for their contributions of knowledge, enthusiasm, encouragement, and support.

Our thanks to Oggi Ogburn and Sam Tremble for their outstanding photographs, and our primary research sources—Joel Whitburn's *Top R&B Singles 1942–1995* and *The New Rolling Stone Encyclopedia of Rock & Roll*, edited by Patricia Romanowski and Holly George-Warren.

And because you believed in us and shared our excitement for this project, special thanks to Clint Holmes, Bruce Bender, and Jim Ellison.

We also thank each and every R&B-Soul artist who ever wrote, produced, recorded, and performed—because without you this book wouldn't have been possible, or necessary.

First, last, and continually, we thank God for our blessings.

Preface

This book was created for one reason—nobody has ever done a trivia book exclusively devoted to R&B-Soul music. So my partner, Sarah Smith, and I decided to do one. Before we put all the time, energy, and research into the project, we did some market testing of our own. Each of us quizzed our friends, family, and coworkers on their knowledge of R&B-Soul music. What we found was real enthusiasm and loads of fun. People—young and old, male and female, Afro-American and white—really got involved and when we asked one trivia question (i.e., name the Supremes' first major hit) everybody always wanted another and came up with one of their own.

So here it is, over five hundred questions and answers about the exciting genre of music known as Rhythm & Blues-Soul. Sarah and I sincerely hope you enjoy it and have lots of fun.

Incidentally, the Supremes' first hit was "Where Did Our Love Go"—number 1, July 11, 1964.

BOBBY BENNETT

The Ultimate
Soul Music
Trivia Book

The Fifties and Sixties

The 1950s were exciting times for all music, but especially Rhythm & Blues. Investors, as well as commercial sponsors, finally started to look at the financial potential of the African-American community, and R&B-Soul radio stations were popping up on the AM dial across the country at a rapid rate. With all of the newly formatted Soul stations available to play the music, the record industry began to sign black artists and produce R&B-Soul music at a pace never before imagined.

It was the fifties that introduced America to such artists as James Brown, Ruth Brown, Sam Cooke, LaVern Baker, Little Richard, B.B. King, Baby Washington, Jackie Wilson, Lloyd Price, and others. Those ten years also produced a multitude of new vocal groups including the Drifters, the Spaniels, Hank Ballard and the Midnighters, Frankie Lymon and the Teenagers, the Platters, the Dells, the Five Keys, the Coasters, the Flamingos, the Moonglows, and the list goes on and on. When we talk about R&B music in America, the fifties must be considered the foundation decade.

During the Sizzling Sixties, Motown, Atlantic, and Stax Records were just a few of the major labels that took Soul music to the next level. Berry Gordy brought a host of talented artists and producers to his Motown house, and music as we knew it was never to be the same. From the many labels created under the Motown banner, stars such as the Supremes, Gladys Knight and the Pips, Stevie Wonder, the Temptations, the Four Tops, Marvin Gaye, the Miracles, and the Jackson 5 were born.

Atlantic Records was another label that created a sound of its own during the sixties with many artists that climbed the ladder to stardom—Aretha Franklin, Otis Redding, Solomon Burke, Ray Charles, Joe Tex, and Don Covay. They all sold a lot of records during the sixties.

In Memphis, Al Bell and Jim Stewart put together the sixties sound of the South with Sam and Dave, Carla Thomas, Booker T. and the MGs, Johnny Taylor, and Rufus Thomas. Isaac Hayes and David Porter became superstar producer-writers and later Hayes became a performer as Stax Records flourished.

Sixties music has been rereleased, rerecorded, sampled, and used on commercials more than any other music of the twentieth century. And sixties Soul still sounds mighty good.

The Fifties and Sixties

Q1. Which duo recorded "I Hope You're Satisfied" and "We're in Love" as Betty and Dupree?

Q2. In the early sixties, Otis Williams (of the Temptations) was engaged to which of these singing divas?
   a. Patti LaBelle
   b. Whitney Houston
   c. Aretha Franklin
   d. Diana Ross

Q3. Who joined the Dells after his stint in the military?
   a. Johnny Carter
   b. Mickey McGill
   c. Marvin Junior
   d. Verne Allison

Q4. Recording artist Tammy Montgomery is best known by what name?

Q5. What superstar male solo artist performed with Harvey and the Moonglows from 1959 through the early sixties?
   a. Nat "King" Cole
   b. Johnny Mathis
   c. Teddy Pendergrass
   d. Marvin Gaye

Q6. Which member of the Dells spent approximately nine months performing with the Moonglows?
   a. Marvin Junior
   b. Phillipe Wynn
   c. Chuck Barksdale
   d. Eugene Record

Q7.   Who played electric guitar for the Isley Brothers before he became a mega star?

The Isley Brothers with author Bobby Bennett (left to right: Rudolph Isley, O'Kelly Isley, Bobby Bennett, and Ronald Isley)

Q8. Which of these jazz musicians (formerly with the Ramsey Lewis Trio) earned credit for the birth of Earth, Wind and Fire in 1969?
   a. Maurice White
   b. Wayne Davis
   c. Bootsy Collins
   d. LaVonne Handy

Q9. The Supremes had their first hit, "Where Did Our Love Go," in 1964. Who were the three members of that group?

Q10. Sammy Strain, former member of the renowned O'Jays, was also a member of which of these groups?
   a. The Capris
   b. The Chi-Lites
   c. Little Anthony and the Imperials
   d. Lee Andrews and the Hearts

Q11. In 1967, what group did Cindy Birdsong leave when she joined the Supremes?

Q12. Which of these singers, before joining the armed forces, was a founding member of the Flamingos?
   a. Lloyd Price
   b. Johnny Carter (of the Dells)
   c. Bubba Knight (of the Pips)
   d. Sam Cooke

Q13. Hiesman Trophy runner-up Ricky Bell's brother led what group to number one with the hit "Tighten Up"?

Q14. Who wrote, and was the first to record, "The Twist"?
   a. Jackie Wilson
   b. Hank Ballard (of Hank Ballard and the Midnighters)
   c. Chubby Checker
   d. Joey Dee

Q15. Who were the four soul-singing ladies Marvin Gaye teamed with for duets?

The Blue-Belles were created with the 1962 top 20 hit,
"I Sold My Heart to the Junkman," but the true
recording artists were the Starlets.

Q16. Who was the male superstar who, in his early years, provided the spoken words on the Moonglow's "Twelve Months of the Year?"

Q17. What male leader of a Motown vocal group was to bring to Berry Gordy's attention the Jackson 5?
   a. Smokey Robinson (of Smokey Robinson and the Miracles)
   b. Levi Stubbs (of the Four Tops)
   c. Bobby Taylor (of Bobby Taylor and the Vancouvers)
   d. David Ruffin (of the Temptations)

Q18. What was Marvin Gaye's first national number 1 hit?
   a. "What's Going On"
   b. "I Heard It Through The Grapevine"
   c. "Sexual Healing"
   d. "Stubborn Kind of Fellow"

Q19. Who was the male solo recording artist from Washington, D.C. lovingly known as "Motormouth?"

Q20. Who, early in his career, cowrote Jackie Wilson's hits, "Reet Petite" and "Lonely Teardrops," before becoming one of the recording industry's major forces?

Q21. The 1956 Top 10 hit "Stranded in the Jungle" was recorded by the Jayhawks; later three of that four-member group formed the nucleus of what group that charted with "The Watusi"?
   a. The Vibrations
   b. The Coasters
   c. The Five Satins
   d. The Drifters

Q22. Gene Pitney wrote "He's a Rebel" and the label credited which of these female vocal groups with the Top 10 hit?
  a. The Blossoms
  b. The Ad Libs
  c. The Crystals
  d. The Orlons

Q23. What artist released "Don't Be a Drop-Out" in 1966 as an example of his civic commitment?

Q24. Discovered by Otis Redding, which one-hit wonder male soul singer recorded "Sweet Soul Music" in 1967?
  a. Tyrone Davis
  b. Arthur Conley
  c. Gregory Abbott
  d. Solomon Burke

Q25. What are the names of the six well-known male stars who recorded as the "Soul Clan" on Atlantic Records?

Q26. Which Motown-based soul group asked, "Do You Love Me"?

Q27. With a band led by Ray Charles, which of these singers recorded "(Mama) He Treats Your Daughter Mean"?
  a. Ruth Brown
  b. Faye Adams
  c. LaVern Baker
  d. Maxine Brown

Born Ray Charles Robinson, this legendary soul singer and composer dropped his last name to avoid confusion with boxer Sugar Ray Robinson.

Q28. Who was the original lead singer of the Drifters?
    a. Clyde McPhatter
    b. Otis Redding
    c. Ben E. King
    d. Eddie Levert

Q29. Who was the top artist of the 1950s with twenty-three gold singles and sixty-five million records sold?
    a. Elvis Presley
    b. James Brown
    c. Fats Domino
    d. Lloyd Price

Q30. What group from Baltimore, Maryland, has the distinction of being called the first R&B vocal group?

Q31. Which artist formed the Band of Gypsies in 1969 with Buddy Miles as drummer?

Q32. What was the name of James Brown's first number 1 R&B hit?
    a. "Please, Please, Please"
    b. "I'll Go Crazy"
    c. "Try Me"
    d. "Think"

Q33. On what label was the Isley Brothers' hit "It's Your Thing" released?
    a. Atlantic
    b. Motown
    c. Capitol
    d. T-Neck

Q34. Who left rock 'n' roll in 1957 to become a minister and returned to secular music in 1964?

Q35. What is the name of the group who were studio musicians on more than 600 Stax/Volt recordings and recorded "Green Onions," "Time Is Tight," and many more hits?

James Brown

Q36. Freddie Gorman was a member of which group that had a hit with "Baby, I'm for Real" (written by Marvin Gaye)?

Q37. "Beep, Beep" or "She Freaks" was heard at a Go-Go club when what artist's song "Bang! Bang!" was playing?
    a. Joe Cuba Sextet
    c. Ramsey Lewis
    c. Young Holt
    d. Ahmad Jamal

Q38. Who were the two singers who took "See Saw" to the Top 10 on the R&B charts—first with his 1965 recording and again with hers in 1969?

Q39. Who were the original members of the Four Tops?

Q40. Who was called the "Ice Man"?

Q41. What were the names of the five Berry Gordy labels popular between 1960–1975?

Q42. The address was 2648 West Grand Boulevard—what was it?
  a. Connie's Headquarters
  b. Graceland
  c. Hitsville, U.S.A. (Motown)
  d. New Bethel Baptist Church

Q43. "Function at the Junction," a 1966 Motown hit, was recorded by which of these artists?
  a. Marv Johnson
  b. Shorty Long
  c. Marvin Gaye
  d. Jr. Walker

Q44. Who was the R&B diva, discovered in the 1950s by legendary soul band leader Johnny Otis, whose early hits included the smash single "All I Could Do Was Cry"?

Q45. Which of these singers was the first young African-American teen idol?
  a. Michael Jackson
  b. Little Anthony
  c. Frankie Lymon
  d. Little Stevie Wonder

Q46. In the early sixties, which singer's smash hit single, "Mother-in-Law," popularized New Orleans style R&B?
  a. Bobby Day
  b. Lee Dorsey
  c. Fats Domino
  d. Ernie K-Doe

Q47. Led by the smooth vocals of Tony Williams, who were the preeminent African-American vocal group of 1955–1960?

Q48. Who were real-life cousins whose first record, "I'm Your Puppet," was a crossover smash?

Q49. Which song gave Frankie Lymon a number 1 R&B single at the age of thirteen?
    a. "I Want You to Be My Girl"
    b. "The ABC's of Love"
    c. "Why Do Fools Fall in Love"
    d. "I Promise to Remember"

Q50. Best known in the music industry for writing hit songs for Fats Domino, Wilson Pickett, and the Dave Clark Five, who struck gold in 1961 with his own hit single "I Like It Like That"?
    a. Gary "U.S." Bonds
    b. Little Milton
    c. Chubby Checker
    d. Chris Kenner

Q51. What's the name of this mega blues man whose first number 1 single in 1951 was called "Three O'Clock Blues"?

Q52. Who was the Texas-born singer who wrote and recorded "Little Bitty Pretty One" and finally hit it big with "Rockin' Robin"?
    a. Clyde McPhatter
    b. Bobby Day
    c. Bobby Lewis
    d. Carroll "Mr. C." Hynson

Q53. Who were the New York preteens who sang about their teacher, "Mr. Lee," in 1957?
    a. The Cookies
    b. The Dixiebelles
    c. The Bobbettes
    d. The Jaynettes

Q54. What group, funded by football great Jim Brown, hit it big with "Grazing in the Grass"?
  a. Fifth Dimension
  b. Friends of Distinction
  c. Rotary Connection
  d. The Four Jewels

Q55. Can you name the singer who recorded "I Don't Want to Cry" and "Any Day Now"?
  a. Chuck Jackson
  b. Walter Jackson
  c. Jermaine Jackson
  d. Jesse L. Jackson

Q56. What 1988 movie brought about the revival of "Do You Love Me"?
  a. *The Big Chill*
  b. *The Mack*
  c. *Dirty Dancing*
  d. *Truck Turner*

Q57. Which of these groups recorded "Stay"?
  a. Earth, Wind and Fire
  b. The Time
  c. Maurice Williams and the Zodiacs
  d. The Fifth Dimension

Q58. If you missed the Motown Revue in Washington, D.C., where could you see the same show in Philadelphia?
  a. The Apollo
  b. The Regal

Valerie Simpson, of the legendary songwriting, performing husband-wife team Ashford and Simpson, is the sister of Ray Simpson, lead vocalist of the Village People.

---

    c. The Uptown

    d. The Howard Theater

Q59. Who was a 1943 Golden Gloves champion, but is better known for performing "I Put a Spell on You"?

    a. Berry Gordy

    b. Screamin' Jay Hawkins

    c. James Brown

    d. Bo Diddley

Q60. Which of these groups recorded the Top 10 R&B *and* pop hit "Mama Said" in 1961?

    a. The Chantels

    b. The Quintones

    b. The Shirelles

    d. The DC 3's

Q61. Can you name the group responsible for the national Top 10 hit "A Lover's Concerto" in 1965?

Q62. What's the name of the group whose hit "Maybe" was written by their lead singer, Arlene Smith?

    a. The Shirelles

    b. The Quintones

    c. The Chantels

    d. The Click-ettes

Q63. Who was called the "Duke of Earl"?

    a. Eugene Record

    b. Gene Chandler

    c. Ray Parker Jr.

    d. Ray Bryant

Q64. Which came first, "Heat Wave" or "Dancing in the Street"—and can you name the group that recorded both songs?

Q65. Highlights of whose career include singing with Mahalia Jackson, and recording the number 1 hit, "Don't You Know"?

Q66. Who predicted in 1963 that "Our Day Will Come"?

Q67. Whose version of "Fever" (only a moderate hit at the time) has since been followed by numerous other versions?
    a. Little Milton's
    b. Little Richard's
    c. Little Anthony's
    d. Little Willie John's

Q68. What group sang the original "In the Still of the Night"?
    a. The "5" Royales
    b. Five Star
    c. The Five Stairsteps
    d. The Five Satins

Q69. Whose "Let It Be Me" with Jerry Butler and her solo hit "The Shoop Shoop Song" assures her a place on the list of R&B's memorable soul sisters?
    a. Brenda Lee Eager
    b. Betty Everett
    c. Thelma Houston
    d. Linda Clifford

Q70. Which group, formed in Gary, Indiana in the early fifties, had national success with "Goodnight Sweetheart, Goodnight"?
    a. The Five Dutones
    b. The Dubs
    c. The Jackson 5
    d. The Spaniels

Q71. Who replaced Florence Ballard in Diana Ross and the Supremes?
    a. Cindy Birdsong
    b. Yvonne Fair
    c. Cindi Mulzac
    d. Blinky Williams

Q72. Who filled in for Tammi Terrell when she couldn't make several recording sessions of hit duos with Marvin Gaye?
   a. Claudette Robinson
   b. Kim Weston
   c. Valerie Simpson
   d. Freda Payne

Q73. Who was the energetic male soul singer who said he won't "take the lady with the skinny legs"?
   a. Curtis Mayfield
   b. Joe Tex
   c. Billy Stewart
   d. Brook Benton

Q74. When Bobby Lewis said "I couldn't sleep at all last night" in 1961, what was he doing?

Q75. Can you name the talented keyboardist and his partners who won a Grammy in 1965 for hanging with "The 'In' Crowd"?

Q76. What long-time music industry super survivor has had his share of hits in his long career, including "Tutti Frutti"?

Q77. Who was the singer born Thomasina Montgomery in Philadelphia, who had a string of hits in the late sixties with a major soul singer?
   a. Kim Weston
   b. Tammi Terrell
   c. Mary Wells
   d. Minnie Riperton

Q78. Who was the major soul singer?
   a. Bill Withers
   b. Teddy Pendergrass
   c. Billy Davis
   d. Marvin Gaye

Q79. Before Aretha Franklin, what Atlantic and Stax record artist was the "Queen of Soul," among whose many hits was the R&B classic "Gee Whiz"?
   a. Mabel John
   b. Carla Thomas
   c. Mavis Staples
   d. Nancy Wilson

Q80. Can you name the youngster—a future soul-music superstar—who shined shoes in front of the Augusta, Georgia, radio station he would later buy?

Q81. Which of these duos made "You Don't Know Like I Know" famous?
   a. Rufus and Carla Thomas
   b. James and Bobby Purify
   c. Sam and Dave
   d. Ashford and Simpson

Q82. In 1969, which of these groups hit the music world with their first single and sold over two million records?

The Jackson 5 (left to right, Marlon, Tito, Randy, Jackie, Michael, and D. J. Sheila Elridge)

    a. The Five Stairsteps
    b. The Jackson 5
    c. The Staple Singers
    d. DeBarge

Q83. What was the name of the song?
    a. "I'll Take You There"
    b. "O-O Child"
    c. "I Want You Back"
    d. "All This Love"

Q84. Can you name the group, formerly known as the Heartbeats, that hit it big with the soul classic "Daddy's Home"?
    a. The Ravens
    b. The Spaniels
    c. The Flamingos
    d. Shep and the Limelites

Q85. In 1969 who was the Simmesport, Louisiana, soul brother who had a number 1 R&B smash called "The Chokin' Kind"?
    a. Jerry Butler
    b. Bobby Womack
    c. Al Green
    d. Joe Simon

Q86. These lovely young ladies were the first female R&B group with a number 1 pop hit and other singles such as: "Mama Said" and "Soldier Boy"; who were they?

Q87. Shirley and Lee, a New Orleans–based duo, had several hit songs, but which one went to number 2 on the R&B charts?
    a. "Tossin' and Turnin'"
    b. "Let the Good Times Roll"
    c. "Try My Love"
    d. "If You Feel the Need"

Q88. Can you name the artists responsible for the soul classic "Hold On, I'm Comin'," which went to number 1 in *Billboard*'s R&B chart in April 1966?

Q89. Who was the one-hit wonder with the monster hit "Barefootin'"?
   a. Johnny "Guitar" Watson
   b. Amos Milburn
   c. Brook Benton
   d. Robert Parker

Q90. Can you name the "blue-eyed soul" quartet from New York City who hit the soul charts in 1967 with "Groovin'"?

Q91. Which smooth singing soul brother from Chicago hit the big time back in 1966 with the R&B classic "Love Is a Hurting Thing"?
   a. Lou Rawls
   b. Jerry Bledsoe
   c. Jerry Butler
   d. Latimore

Q92. Who was the singer, a native of Detroit and a former member of the Falcons, who recorded "Mustang Sally" a year before Wilson Pickett?
   a. Sam Cooke
   b. Sir Mack Rice
   c. Gene Chandler
   d. Fats Domino

Q93. Can you name the blue-eyed brothers who hit it big in the record world in 1965, but lost that loving feeling in 1968 and went their separate ways?
   a. Surface
   b. Yarbrough & Peoples
   c. The Righteous Brothers
   d. Brothers Johnson

Q94. Who was the great man of soul—a onetime member of Johnny Jenkins and the Pinetoppers—who went on to achieve superstar status with hits such as "Respect" and "(Sitting on the) Dock of the Bay"?

Q95. When Otis Redding was killed in a tragic plane crash in 1967, four members of which of these famous bands were also killed in that crash?
   a. Kool and the Gang
   b. Bar-Kays
   c. GAP Band
   d. Atlantic Starr

Q96. Barbara Acklin hit the big time with her 1968 recording of "Love Makes a Woman," and she was married to what heart-throb lead singer of a famous group?
   a. Dennis Edwards
   b. Eugene Record
   c. Tommy Hunt
   d. Ray Payne

Q97. What was the name of his group?

Q98. What group included Merry Clayton and Minnie Riperton, among others, and was named for the artist whom they accompanied?

Q99. "Voice Your Choice," a 1965 hit, was made popular by which Chicago-based vocal group that came together at the Greater Harvest Baptist church?
   a. The Ran-Dells
   b. The Raindrops
   c. The Ram-Rods
   d. The Radiants

Members of Friends of Distinction included Harry Elston, Floyd Butler, Barbara Love, and Jessica Cleaves (who later joined Earth, Wind and Fire).

Q100. Which famous R&B doo-wop group of the fifties had a lead singer named Pookie Hudson?

Q101. "Lawdy Miss Clawdy" was the first of four number 1 R&B hits for which of these R&B pioneers?
   a. Fats Domino
   b. Lloyd Price
   c. Clyde McPhatter
   d. Little Richard

Q102. Which of these British rock groups had the hit "A Whiter Shade of Pale" that crossed over to the R&B audience?
   a. The Animals
   b. The Yardbirds
   c. Procul Harum
   d. Dave Clark Five

Q103. Which jazz funk trio featured two members who formerly played with the Ramsey Lewis Trio and whose one major hit was "Soulful Strut"?
   a. The Crusaders
   b. Young-Holt Unlimited
   c. Raydio
   d. Brass Construction

Q104. Who performed "When a Man Loves a Woman," a 1966 smash hit number 1 song?
   a. Otis Redding
   b. Tyrone Davis
   c. Percy Sledge
   d. William Bell

Q105. Jimmy Beaumont was the lead singer of the Sky-liners, a Pittsburgh-based blue-eyed soul group that charted which major *Billboard* hit?
   a. "Call Me"
   b. "Since I Don't Have You"
   c. "16 Candles"
   d. "You're a Big Girl Now"

Q106. To which popular R&B vocal group did Tommy Hunt, whose later solo effort, "Human"—a moderate success—belong?
   a. The Intruders
   b. The Flamingos
   c. The Whispers
   d. The Valentinos

Q107. Who sang "Every Little Bit Hurts" and "When I'm Gone"?
   a. Kim Weston
   b. Brenda Holloway
   c. Mary Wells
   d. Diane Love

Q108. What group recorded "What Kind of Fool (Do You Think I Am)"?
   a. Crown Heights Affairs
   b. The Choice Four
   c. The Tams
   d. The Yeomans

Q109. Who is still remembered for his 1957 hit "Chances Are"?

Q110. What is the title of Lloyd Price's number 1 R&B and pop hit of 1959? (Hint: Ruth Brown and Adam Wade starred in a Broadway production of the same name.)

In 1962 these soon-to-be superstars recorded four flop singles on the Motown label including "Mind Over Matter" and "I'll Love You Till I Die" under the name of the Pirates. The group, later known as the Temptations, was made up of Eddie Kendricks, Paul Williams, Melvin Franklin, Otis Williams, and Elbridge Bryant.

Q111. Not discouraged by his unsuccessful audition for the Moonglows, this soulful tenor went on to join another group for a winning year ("There Goes My Baby," "Save the Last Dance For Me," etc.). Who was he?

Q112. What was the name of the group?

Q113. Who released "What Becomes of the Broken Hearted?" on Motown's Soul label?

Q114. What was the name of the Temptations' 1969 number 1 R&B and pop hit?
    a. "My Girl"
    b. "I Can't Get Next to You"
    c. "Papa Was a Rolling Stone"
    d. "Just My Imagination"

Q115. Who is credited with choreography for the Supremes, the Spinners, the Contours, and the Temptations?
    a. Honey Cole
    b. Cholly Atkins
    c. Earl "Fatha" Hines
    d. Gregory Hines

Q116. Who is the Motor-City–based artist who wrote "Money (That's What I Want)" and cowrote "I Wish It Would Rain," "Psychedelic Shack," and "I Heard It Through the Grapevine"?

Q117. "So Much in Love" was a jumbo hit for what group in 1963?
    a. The Fiestas
    b. The Wanderers
    c. The Tymes
    d. The Temprees

Q118. In the late fifties "Talk To Me, Talk To Me" was a hit for which gifted vocalist?
    a. Brook Benton
    b. Little Willie John
    c. Dinah Washington
    d. O. C. Smith

Smokey Robinson (right) with author Bobby Bennett

Q119. Who was Berry Gordy's superstar onetime brother-in-law?
  a. Marvin Gaye
  b. Jackie Wilson
  c. Smokey Robinson
  d. David Ruffin

Q120. Which soulful group is readily remembered for the fun songs "Searching," "Young Blood," and "Yakety Yak"?
  a. The Contours
  b. The Time
  c. The Coasters
  d. The Jayhawks

Q121. Among their hits were "Devil or Angel" and "One Mint Julep." Who was this group?

Q122. Who sang "Eddie My Love" in 1956?
   a. The Teen Queens
   b. The Toys
   c. The Chiffons
   d. Ruby and the Romantics

Q123. In the fifties, the Penguins had the million seller "Earth Angel"; who cowrote that hit?
   a. Sam Cooke
   b. Barrett Strong
   c. Nat "King" Cole
   d. Jesse Belvin

Q124. Whose 1965 release of "The 'In' Crowd" was in the R&B *and* Pop Top 20, and twelve years later his "Drift Away" went to the Top 5 on the pop charts?
   a. Bobby Womack
   b. Adam Wade
   c. Lenny Williams
   d. Dobie Gray

Q125. Who recorded "Betty Lou Got a New Pair of Shoes" after he recorded "Do You Wanna Dance"?

Q126. This 1967 hit soul duet sang "It Takes Two"; who were the two?

Q127. What hitsville soulful group (one lady and three men) had hits with "Darling Baby" and "Heaven Must Have Sent You"?
   a. The Monitors
   b. The Elgins
   c. Gladys Knight and the Pips
   d. The Miracles

Q128. Whose late fifties hits, "Short Fat Fanny" and "Bony Moronie" inspired comparisons to Little Richard?
   a. Joe Williams
   b. Maurice Williams

    c. Larry Williams

    d. Otis Williams

Q129. Whose wellspring of "Still Water (Love)" and "Quiet Storm" won't be "Fading Away" from the hearts and minds of soul music for years to come, "Ain't That Peculiar"?

Q130. Which Supreme sang lead on "Buttered Popcorn"?

Q131. The lyric "I got all the riches, baby, one man can claim" is from what all-time great hit?

Q132. "The Court of Love" and "The Beginning of My End" were two of the more popular songs recorded by which Washington, D.C.–based soul quartet back in 1968?

    a. Special Delivery

    b. The Unifics

    c. The Ascots

    d. Pure Soul

Q133. The Tune Weavers, a four-person vocal group from Woburn, Massachusetts, were truly one-hit wonders; what is the name of that hit?

    a. "Happy, Happy Birthday Baby"

    b. "Tra La La La La"

    c. "Sweet Sixteen"

    d. "Baby Get It On"

Q134. What male and female songbirds from Washington, D.C., made a career singing about love, such as "Let's Fall in Love"?

    a. Mickey and Sylvia

    b. Ashford and Simpson

    c. Marvin and Tammy

    d. Peaches and Herb

Q135. What is the name of this fabulous soul group that had twelve top 10 singles (eight R&B and four UK),

Singer, producer, and songwriter Curtis Mayfield

including "Rockin' Roll Baby," and Russell Thompkins Jr. as the lead singer since 1968?

   a. Blue Magic
   b. The Intruders
   c. The Whispers
   d. The Stylistics

Q136. Betty Jean Champion had a number 1 R&B record called "Make Me Yours" in July 1967; what was Betty's stage name?

   a. Bette Davis
   b. Betty Wright
   c. Betty Everett
   d. Bettye Swann

Q137. Whitney Houston's mother, Cissy Houston, was a member of what group that sometimes backed stars such as Aretha Franklin and Elvis Presley?
   a. Sweet Sable
   b. Sweet Inspirations
   c. Sweet Obsession
   d. Sweet Thunder

Q138. "C.C. Rider" and "What Am I Living For" were hits in the fifties for which veteran soul artist?
   a. Chuck Willis
   b. Bobby Freeman
   c. Ivory Joe Hunter
   d. Johnny Ace

Q139. What Philadelphia vocal group of the fifties who sang "When You Dance" is probably better known for the unique headdresses they wore on stage than for their music?

Q140. What male/female vocal group put together by Isaac Hayes and David Porter back in the late sixties enjoyed success on the Stax label with hits like "I'll Understand" and "The Sweeter He Is"?

Q141. "Hypnotized," a major R&B smash in the spring and summer of 1967, was performed by what beautiful soul sister from New Jersey?
   a. Millie Jackson
   b. Etta James
   c. Dionne Warwick
   d. Linda Jones

Q142. The Impressions singing group produced two men who went on to tremendous solo careers; who are they?

Q143. Which husband-and-wife team were members of the Fifth Dimension?

Q144. What famous female singer, her sister, and aunt were once part of a gospel trio called the Gospelaires?

Q145. "This Bitter Earth" and "Baby, You've Got What It Takes" were only two of which hall-of-fame lady's hits?
   a. Eartha Kitt
   b. Dinah Washington
   c. Pearl Bailey
   d. Ella Fitzgerald

Q146. Justine Washington was her real name and "That's How Heartaches Are Made" was her biggest hit; what was her stage name?

Q147. In 1958, which artist had a major hit with "Willie and the Hand Jive"?
   a. Shuggie Otis
   b. Johnny Otis
   c. Tony Payne
   d. Otis Smith

Q148. Who was this late legendary R&B giant who replaced Clyde McPhatter with Billy Ward's Dominoes and was the godfather of Jody Watley?
   a. Joe Simon
   b. Joe Turner
   c. Jackie Wilson
   d. Brook Benton

Q149. "Color Him Father," a 1969 Grammy Award–winning R&B song, was performed by what Washington, D.C., soul group?
   a. The Unifics
   b. Special Delivery
   c. The Soul Searchers
   d. The Winstons

Q150. Who took a "Hundred Pounds of Clay" and made a hit record?
   a. Bobby McFerrin

    b. Gene McDaniels
    c. Willie Mitchell
    d. Brian McKnight

Q151. What are the names of the three R&B number 1 songs Clyde McPhatter enjoyed during his Hall of Fame career?

Q152. "Backfield in Motion" was a hit record produced by Gene Chandler for which soul duo?
    a. Sam and Dave
    b. Mel and Tim
    c. Ashford and Simpson
    d. McFadden and Whitehead

Q153. "Cissy Strut" and "Sophisticated Cissy" were hits by which instrumental group from New Orleans?
    a. Whistle
    b. B. T. Express
    c. Pieces of a Dream
    d. The Meters

Q154. Sam and Dave enjoyed success during the sixties with what two R&B songs?

Q155. What group is best known for one record—"Wooly Bully"?
    a. Shades of Blue
    b. Sam the Sham and the Pharaohs

Sam Moore and Dave Prater, later known as Sam and Dave, met when Moore was emceeing an amateur-night contest in a Miami club and Prater, who was performing Jackie Wilson's smash "Doggin' Around," forgot the words. Sam coached Dave through the rest of the song.

---

    c. The Shangrilas

    d. Technotronic

Q156. What well-known artist, joined by his brothers early in his career, achieved a measure of success "Lookin' for a Love" as the Valentinos?

Q157. Who was the Chicago songbird who recorded under the name of Andrea Davis on Chess Records in 1966 and died of cancer in 1979?

    a. LaVern Baker

    b. Sarah Vaughn

    c. Minnie Riperton

    d. Dakota Staton

Q158. Who formed a group called the Matadors in 1954, later changed its name, then he and and the group miraculously gained stardom?

Q159. Who began his dynamic soul music career in the fifties that has earned him many accolades, including the 1992 Grammy Lifetime Achievement Award?

Q160. What late singer had several hits in the early sixties written by Smokey Robinson, including "Two Lovers"?

Q161. Which group is remembered for "A Little Bit of Soap"?

    a. The Jarmels

    b. The Chambers Brothers

    c. The Artistics

    d. The Solitaires

Originally the Primettes, they could have been named the Darleens, the Sweet P's, the Melodees, the Royaltones, or the Jewelettes—but they became the Supremes.

Q162. What lady demanded "R-e-s-p-e-c-t"?

Q163. Who simply said, "It's My Party"?
  a. Carolyn Smith
  b. Lesley Gore
  c. Claudine Clark
  d. Claudja Barry

Q164. What was the name of the Miracles' 1960 hit that remained number 1 on the R&B charts for eight weeks?
  a. "You've Really Got a Hold on Me"
  b. "The Tears of a Clown"
  c. "Bad Girl"
  d. "Shop Around"

Q165. Which Latin/jazz musician enjoyed some R&B and commercial success in the late sixties with "No Matter What Shape (Your Stomach's In)"?
  a. Willie Bobo
  b. Ahmad Jamal
  c. Les McCann
  d. Cal Tjader

Q166. What Harlem group sang "Please Say You Want Me"?

Q167. The Marvelettes had many songs in the Top 100, but only one number 1; what was the name of their number 1 hit?

Q168. What artist, at eleven years of age, played piano on Jesse Belvin's recording of "Goodnight My Love"?
  a. Little Richard
  b. Huey "Piano" Smith
  c. Barry White
  d. Ray Charles

Q169. "Little Green Apples" took what singer high on both the R&B and Pop charts in 1968?

Q170. In 1968 this South African musician had a monster R&B and Pop hit; who is he and what was the song?

Q171. What is the name of his ex-wife (also onetime wife of a well-known activist) and her 1967 Top 10 R&B hit?

Q172. The Temptations had four number 1 R&B hits in 1966; what are the names of two of them?

Q173. Which Chicago-based quartet did a very successful cover of the Beatles' "Day Tripper"?
   a. The Vibrations
   b. The Valentinos
   c. The Velvelettes
   d. The Vontastics

Q174. What rocking party band had many hits during the sixties and seventies, and their first hit was "Shotgun"?

Q175. What integrated group had two R&B Top 10 hits in 1957, "Come Go With Me" and "Whispering Bells"?
   a. The Crests
   b. The Del-Vikings
   c. The Doves
   d. The Harp-Tones

Q176. Over the years, their 1968 recording of "Girl Watcher" has become a classic beach record; what is the name of the group?
   a. One Way
   b. The O'Kaysions
   c. Silver Convention
   d. The Silhouettes

Q177. What R&B veteran is a member of a famous New Orleans musical family, and in 1966 had a solo smash entitled, "Tell It Like It Is"?

Q178. Wanda Young, a sometime lead songer of Motown's Marvelettes, was married to which member of Smokey Robinson and the Miracles?
   a. Ronnie White
   b. Pete Moore

    c. Bobby Rodgers

    d. William Robinson

Q179. Whose real name was Autry DeWalt and was known for up-tempo dance music, including the soul classic "Come See About Me"?

    a. Amos Milburn

    b. Junior Parker

    c. Jr. Jackson

    d. Jr. Walker

Q180. "Splish Splash," he was taking a bath; what is the name of the bather?

Q181. In 1954, what Los Angeles–based soul quartet had a gigantic number 1 R&B record, which has over the years sold an estimated 10 million copies called "Earth Angel"?

    a. The Duo-Tones

    b. The Coasters

    c. The Orioles

    d. The Penguins

Q182. The collaboration of Booker T. and the MGs and Wilson Pickett created what soul classic back in 1965?

    a. "Don't Knock My Love"

    b. "In the Midnight Hour"

    c. "634–5789"

    d. "Engine No. 9"

Q183. What lady sang some serious blues and in 1953 was on top of the music world with two number 1 R&B songs, including her best-known hit, "Shake a Hand"?

    a. Ruth Brown

    b. LaVern Baker

    c. Faye Adams

    d. Big Maybelle

Q184. When you talk about the early years of R&B you have to include what horn-rimmed-glasses–wearing, rectangular-guitar–playing genius?

Q185. Who found his thrill on "Blueberry Hill"?

Q186. Whose first hit "Chapel of Love" was their biggest hit?
    a. The Ronettes
    b. The Dixie Cups
    c. The Chiffons
    d. The Buttercups

Q187. Whose jump to Rhythm and Blues stardom happened with the 1956 release of a song called "Honky Tonk"?
    a. Mose Allison
    b. Eddie "Lockjaw" Davis
    c. Jr. Walker
    d. Bill Doggett

Q188. Who was the soul brother who tried boxing before he hit the charts in 1961 with the two hits "Ya Ya" and "Do Re Mi"?
    a. Dr. John
    b. Dr. Hook
    c. Lee Dorsey
    d. Al Hurt

Q189. "Shirley, Shirley, Bo Burley, Banana Fana, Fo Fairley" were some of the lyrics from the 1965 hit, "The Name Game"; who sang it?
    a. Doris Troy
    b. Baby Washington
    c. Shirley Murdoch
    d. Shirley Ellis

Q190. What group was already on the road to success when they exploded with their biggest hit ever, "Aquarius/Let the Sunshine In"?

Q191. In 1953, the Royal Sons Gospel Quintet changed their name and went to the top of the R&B charts with two number-1 hits, "Baby Don't Do It" and "Help Me Somebody"; what is the name of these R&B pioneers?
    a. The "5" Royales

b. The Royalettes
c. The Royal Kings
d. The Royaltones

Q192. What three artists recorded these dance craze songs: "The Madison Time"; "Mashed Potato Time"; and "Do the Funky Chicken"?

Q193. How many number 1 R&B hits did Diana Ross and the Supremes chart?

Q194. In 1969 "Oh Happy Day" was a giant hit for which group?
a. Staple Singers
b. The Edwin Hawkins Singers
c. Sounds of Blackness
d. Kirk Franklin and the Family

Q195. "My Whole World Ended" was whose hit solo debut?

Q196. In 1953, "Honey Hush" was a hit for which "Big" Rock and Roll Hall of Fame singer?
a. Joe Hunter
b. Joe Turner
c. David Peaston
d. Toussaint McCall

Q197. "You'll Never Walk Alone," a 1954 R&B chart-topping classic, catapulted what performer to stardom?

Q198. "Baby Scratch My Back" was the one and only R&B number 1 record for which artist in 1966?
a. Don "Sugarcane" Harris
b. Slim Harpo
c. Wilbert Harrison
d. Hawkeye Whitney

Q199. "Kansas City" was which soul singer's destination in 1959?
a. Lloyd Price
b. Fats Domino

    c. Wilbert Harrison

    d. Eric Payne

Q200. The album "Hot Buttered Soul" went solid gold in 1969; how many long songs were on the album?

Q201. What was the name of the artist who recorded the album?

Q202. Singer-songwriter Bobby Hebb is best known for what 1966 smash?

Q203. What New Orleans pianist/singer's moment of national stardom came in 1960 with his recording of "Ooh Poo Pah Doo"?

    a. Clarence "Frogman" Henry

    b. Allen Toussaint

    c. Jesse Hill

    d. Solomon Burke

Q204. Who was simply known as "Lady Day"?

Q205. Next to James Brown, what artist was probably the most popular African-American entertainer of the mid-sixties with hits such as "These Arms of Mine"?

Q206. Ruth Lee Jones was one of the most popular African-American female singers of the fifties; what was her stage name?

Q207. Which Chi-Town–based group provided backup vocals for Major Lance and in 1966 had their own R&B Top 10 hit with "I'm Gonna Miss You"?

    a. The Enchanters

    b. The Independents

    c. The Ebonys

    d. The Artistics

Q208. Her career began in 1950 and she was an early superstar of R&B. "Release Me" and "And I Love Him" were two of her hits from the sixties. Who was she?

The Dixie Cups hit the top of the charts in 1964 with
"Chapel of Love." Their manager, Joe Jones, had a
1960 Top 5 single: "You Talk Too Much."

Q209. In early 1963, what quartet rose to the Top 10 with
"Tell Him"? (Two members of this group also teamed
to become parents of a son, known to the world as
songwriter/producer L. A. Reid.)
   a. Essex
   b. The Elgins
   c. The Exciters
   d. Exposé

    c. The GAP Band

    d. The Sugarhill Gang

Q218. Who recorded "I Feel Sanctified"?

Q219. Which soul group had one big hit, "Rock the Boat"?
    a. The Hues Corporation
    b. The Jets
    c. The Independents
    d. The Superlatives

Q220. Whose reward for her role in the Broadway production of *Black and Blue* was a Tony Award, thirty-seven years after her fifties hit, "5–10–15 Hours"?
    a. Ruth Brown
    b. Sarah Vaughn
    c. Lena Horne
    d. Bessie Smith

Q221. What "Master Blaster" superstar wrote "Tell Me Something Good," a Top 10 hit for Rufus?

Q222. What elementary and junior-high schoolmate of Frankie Lymon and Leslie Uggams replaced Frankie with the Teenagers and in 1972 released "Troglodyte" with his own group?

Q223. "Good Loving Don't Come Easy" and "It Don't Cost You Nothing" are which "Solid" duo's song writing or vocal hits?

Q224. In 1973, then Howard University jazz studies professor Donald Byrd founded what group who later were "Walking in Rhythm"?

Q225. Before he became known as Kashif, he was a keyboardist with which group when they recorded "Do It ('Til You're Satisfied)" and other hits?
    a. B. T. Express
    b. Brass Construction

c. New Birth

d. The Brothers Johnson

Q226. What smooth male soul singer was rewarded with a Grammy in 1972 for the mega hit "Me and Mrs. Jones"?

Q227. Which "royal" performer hit the charts in 1971 with a song called "Groove Me"?

a. King Floyd

b. Ben E. King

c. George Duke

d. King Curtis

Q228. Who was discovered while working as a cleanup lady at a Philadelphia recording studio, and whose first recording "Shame" was a major hit?

a. Deniece Williams

b. Cheryl Lynn

c. Patrice Rushen

d. Evelyn "Champagne" King

Q229. Which superstar female song stylist was born Yvette Marie Stevens, and whose stage name means "fire"?

a. Chaka Khan

b. Queen Latifah

c. Ta-Ta Vega

d. Sade

Q230. Harry Wayne Casey is the leader of which band that hit it big in 1975 with "Get Down Tonight"?

Q231. In the "Good Times," the starting line-up was: Bernard Edwards, Nile Rodgers, Norma Jean, and Luci Martin. What was the group?

Q232. What Sagittarius tenor could (and did) "Boogie Down" with the best of 'em?

Q233. Who told us "Mama Told Me (Not to Come)," but with more than fifteen back-to-back hits, they couldn't stay home?

Ronnie Dyson of Top 10 hit fame with "(If You Let Me Make Love to You Then) Why Can't I Touch You?" had a leading role in the Broadway musical Hair.

Q234. Who are the eight sisters and brothers from Minneapolis; Chicago's four brothers and one sister (another brother came later); Grand Rapid's four brothers and a sister; and four brothers from New Bedford, Massachusetts, all youthful hit-making families? (None are the Jacksons.)

Q235. If you had dinner with the "Queen of Soul," the "Godfather of Soul," and the "Master of Reggae," who would be seated at your table?

Q236. Margie Joseph teamed with which group to do a winning rendition of "What's Come Over Me"?
   a. Black Ivory
   b. Blue Magic
   c. The Reddings
   d. L.T.D.

Q237. What artists all had hits about the great state of Georgia with: "Rainy Night in Georgia"; Midnight Train to Georgia"; and "Georgia On My Mind"?

Q238. Who recorded "Can I Change My Mind" and "Turn Back the Hands of Time"?
   a. Solomon Burke
   b. Lloyd Price
   c. Tyrone Davis
   d. Eddie Floyd

Q239. Whose first album *First Take* was a hit the first *and* second time it was released in 1969 and 1972?

Q240. Who asked, "Will It Go Round in Circles"?
   a. Buddy Miles
   b. Ray Charles

    c. Billy Preston

    d. George Benson

Q241. In 1971, who was the first African-American composer of a movie soundtrack to win an Academy Award?

    a. Michael Jackson

    b. Isaac Hayes

    c. Lionel Richie

    d. Quincy Jones

Q242. What was the name of the movie?

Q243. Aretha Franklin ("Sweet Bitter Love"), Peaches and Herb ("Let's Fall in Love"), Gladys Knight and the Pips ("Giving Up"), and David Ruffin ("Walk Away From Love"), all knew him (and his song writing)—but it wasn't until 1975 (and "The Hustle") that what artist became a household name?

    a. Marvin Gaye

    b. William DeVaughn

    c. Billy Stewart

    d. Van McCoy

Q244. If you think "You Should Be Dancin'," but you're just "Stayin' Alive," you remember which group?

    a. The Stylistics

    b. The Bee Gees

    c. The Righteous Brothers

    d. Chic

Q245. When we heard her multi-octave voice on Stevie Wonder's composition "Lovin' You," who jumped on a fast track up the charts?

Q246. General Johnson had great songwriting abilities—the Honey Cone's "Want Ads" and Clarence Carter's "Patches"—but his group's most successful effort was in 1970 with "Give Me Just a Little More Time"; what was the name of his group?

a. 8th Day
b. Chairmen of the Board
c. The Elgins
d. Anacostia

Q247. There's been an abundance of "rain" songs; who are the artist(s) who recorded: "I Wish It Would Rain," "In the Rain," "Walkin' in the Rain With the One I Love," and "Raindrops"?

Q248. Who recorded "Misty Blue"?
a. Marie Kelley
b. R. Kelly
c. Dorothy Moore
d. Jackie Moore

Q249. Who recorded on the Philly Groove label, and one of their hits was the mind-blowing "Didn't I"?
a. The Intruders
b. Hall and Oates
c. The Delfonics
d. The Independents

Q250. Las Vegas superstar Lola Falana was married to a member of which group?
a. DeBarge
b. Black Ivory
c. Guy
d. Tavares

Q251. In the early seventies, his group was the opening act for the Jackson 5, in the late seventies, he wrote a hit for Kenny Rogers, and by the mid-eighties, he'd won an Oscar for a number 1 song from the film *White Nights;* who is he?
a. Lionel Richie
b. Smokey Robinson
c. Dennis Coffey
d. Luther Vandross

Q252. Who is the "Sophisticated Lady" who earned a lot of "Our Love"?

Q253. The Drifters sang "Up on the Roof," but who recorded "Up the Ladder to the Roof"?
   a. The Marvelettes
   b. The Supremes
   c. The Vontastics
   d. A Taste of Honey

Q254. Who became a hit nationwide with his reggae-influenced "I Can See Clearly Now"?
   a. Johnny Nash
   b. Taj Mahal
   c. Jimmy Cliff
   d. Shabba Ranks

Q255. Who are the hit makers of "Three Times a Lady," "That Lady," "Lady Love," and "Special Lady"?

Q256. Who was a one-hit wonder with "Kung-Fu Fighting," which was number 1 here and abroad?
   a. Carl Carlton
   b. Carl Lewis
   c. Carl Douglas
   d. Carl Anderson

Q257. Who sang "Ain't No Woman Like the One I Got"?

Q258. In the late seventies, whose "Trying To Love Two" was a fast favorite?
   a. Smokey Robinson
   b. William Bell
   c. Wilson Pickett
   d. Charlie Foxx

Q259. What Grammy Award–winning musician's 1976 recording of "This Masquerade" was a number 1 hit on the R&B, pop, and jazz charts?

Q260. These flamboyant ladies asked the question "What Can I Do For You"?
   a. The Pointer Sisters
   b. En Vogue
   c. Martha and the Vandellas
   d. LaBelle

Q261. Tony Silvester, Luther Simmons, and Cuba Gooding formed what smooth soul trio of the seventies whose big hit was "Everybody Plays the Fool"?

Q262. What successful Jersey City, New Jersey, R&B doo-wop group was named after a section of New York City?

Q263. Before his musical career took off, which superstar performer of the late sixties and early seventies was a disc jockey at KSOL radio?
   a. Sir Mack Rice
   b. Jr. Walker
   c. Sly (of the Family Stone)
   d. Larry Graham

Q264. What Philadelphia soul group had a great deal of success in the seventies with a string of hits that included "Betcha By Golly, Wow" and "You Are Every-thing"?

Q265. In 1979, which group came together and through their efforts helped to make rap music became part of the pop music scene?
   a. Run-DMC
   b. Public Enemy
   c. Sugarhill Gang
   d. The Ghetto Boys

Q266. "Who's Makin' Love" propelled which bluesy soul singer into music stardom?

    a. Garnet Mims

    b. Tyrone Davis

    c. Johnnie Taylor

    d. Rufus Thomas

Q267. Always a crowd pleaser on stage and a definite favorite on record, what fabulous soul man became a Muslim minister in 1972, following a great singing career?

    a. Little Richard

    b. Solomon Burke

    c. Joe Tex

    d. Dave "Baby" Cortez

Q268. Ike and Tina Turner received a 1971 best R&B vocal performance Grammy for which crossover smash?

    a. "Proud Mary"

    b. "Twist and Shout"

    c. "Respect"

    d. "Satisfaction"

Q269. Who is the talented soul band that asked the musical question, "Why Can't We Be Friends"?

    a. Mandrill

    b. War

    c. Midnite Star

    d. Abaco Dream

Q270. What group started as the backup band for the Falcons when Wilson Pickett was the lead singer, and in 1971 became stars with the number 1 R&B single "Funky Worm," their first taste of musical success?

    a. MFSB

    b. Ohio Players

    c. War

    d. Midnight Star

Actually formed in 1962 by Harold Brown and Howard Scott, this popular soul band played under the name of the Creators. They also once backed Hall-of-Fame football star Deacon Jones. The band took the name War when Eric Burdon joined their lineup for a short time.

Q271. What group started as the Mascots but later took the name of a popular Cleveland disc jockey before rising to stardom?

Q272. Eugene Record was the lead singer of which popular soul group?
   a. The Moments
   b. The Platters
   c. The Chi-Lites
   d. The Impressions

Q273. What creative funkmaster founded one of the most prolific funk rock bands of our times, producing and singing numerous hits, including "Flashlight," "Aqua Boogie," and "One Nation Under a Groove"?

Q274. Minnie Riperton was once the lead singer of Rotary Connection, and later a member of which backup group?
   a. Rufus
   b. Sweet Inspirations
   b. Wonderlove
   d. The Ikettes

Q275. In 1975, who rode the "Love Rollercoaster" to number 1 success on the pop and R&B charts?
   a. The Silos
   b. Shirley & Co.
   c. Ohio Players
   d. Tribe

Q276. A native of Houston, Texas, what vocalist/keyboardist has done it all, including touring in 1975 as the opening act for the Rolling Stones?
  a. Billy Ocean
  b. Billy Stewart
  c. Billy Paul
  d. Billy Preston

Q277. Whose number 1 hit "We Are Family" became the theme song for the 1979 World Champion Pittsburgh Pirates baseball team?
  a. The Pointer Sisters
  b. LaBelle
  c. Sister Sledge
  d. The Soul Children

Q278. Which family's presence in the Soul/R&B/pop arena was short-lived, but had a great impact with "Too Late To Turn Back Now"?
  a. The Sylvers
  b. Cornelius Brothers and Sister Rose
  c. The Chambers Brothers
  d. The Jones Girls

Q279. February 19, 1940, is the birthdate of two members of what group that enjoyed number 1 R&B and pop status with "Tears of a Clown"?

Q280. Rick James sang, "I love you _____"?
  a. Baby Ruth
  b. Mary Jane
  c. Katy Did
  d. Lollipop

Q281. Stevie Wonder won Grammy Awards for Album of the Year (as producer and as performer) in 1973 and 1974; what was the name of either album?

Superstar Stevie Wonder

Q282. Who, whether soulfully crooning, gallantly handing
out roses, or preaching the word, is always winning
his audience?

Q283. Which native of Newark, New Jersey, hit the top of the
pop charts with "I Will Survive"?
   a. Gloria Gaynor
   b. Gloria Lynn
   c. Gloria Naylor
   d. Gloria Johnson

Q284. What six-member soul band, from England, had the
ears of America with "You Sexy Thing"?

Q285. What was the name of the *Good Times* TV show
character portrayed by Janet Jackson?

Did you know that Janet Jackson, the youngest member of the music industry's best-known family, once aspired to be a jockey?

Q286. What gifted soul artist, best known for his winning duets with a Howard University classmate, sang the theme song for TV's *Maude*?

Q287. What was the name of his classmate?

Q288. "I Love You for All Seasons" was one of two Top 20 R&B hits for which Washington, D.C., trio?
  a. The Four Jewels
  b. The Toys
  c. The Fuzz
  d. The D.C. 3's

Q289. What 1975 single was responsible for a brand-new radio format?

Q290. A few days for gold and a few months for platinum was "Right on Time" for what group?

Q291. Whose 1972 monumental hit was "(If Loving You Is Wrong) I Don't Want To Be Right"?

Q292. Which soulful R&B singer soared to popularity by virtue of his relationship with "Mrs. Jones"?
  a. Billy Preston
  b. Billy Paul
  c. Billy Davis
  d. Bill Withers

Q293. "Love To Love You Baby" was the first hit for what sexy disco diva?

Q294. Which lovely lady was the only continuing member of the Supremes from beginning to end?
  a. Diana Ross

    b. Cindy Birdsong
    c. Mary Wilson
    d. Florence Ballard

Q295. Which soul brother said "War, what is it good for" back in 1970?
    a. Steely Dan
    b. Terry Steele
    c. Wilson Pickett
    d. Edwin Starr

Q296. Discovered by Jermaine Jackson, what group's first record, "There'll Never Be," was their biggest hit?
    a. DeBarge
    b. Switch
    c. Tavares
    d. The Sylvers

Q297. Johnny Nash, a handsome and talented Houston, Texas, native, was backed by Bob Marley's Wailers on what 1972 hit single?

Q298. Big Al Wilson made a record in 1973 using what phrase that describes an elementary school activity?

Q299. Who was Mrs. Clarence Carter for a time, but really established a name for herself with the 1976 R&B number 1 "Young Hearts Run Free"?
    a. Candi Shannon
    b. Barbara Mason
    c. Candi Staton
    d. Laura Lee

Q300. What family group, based out of Chicago, created three number 1 R&B hits between 1972 and 1975, including "If You're Ready Come Go With Me"?

Q301. What are the names of the other two number ones?

Q302. The theme song from *Which Way Is Up,* from the movie starring Richard Pryor, was the only number 1 song from which group?
  a. The Five Stairsteps
  b. Stargard
  c. The Starlets
  d. Starpoint

Q303. "Nathan Jones" was the title of a 1971 hit from what female soul group?
  a. The Orlons
  b. The Ronettes
  b. The Supremes
  d. The Pointer Sisters

Q304. They call this South Carolina–born former lead singer of Kool and the Gang J. T.; what is his name?
  a. Johnnie Taylor
  b. Joe Tex
  c. James Taylor
  d. Junior Tucker

Q305. "Disco Inferno," a 1977 hit from the movie *Saturday Night Fever,* was recorded by which group?
  a. Lisa Lisa and Cult Jam
  b. The Trammps
  c. The Tymes
  d. Tony! Toni! Toné!

Q306. What Detroit-born singer replaced Smokey Robinson in the Miracles in 1972?
  a. Billy Griffin
  b. Gary Payne
  c. Bobby Gregg
  d. Lou Courtney

Q307. "One Monkey Don't Stop No Show, Part 1" and "Stick Up" were songs from which talented female trio?
  a. Salt-n-Pepa
  b. Taste of Honey

    c. Honey Cone

    d. Hot Chocolate

Q308. Donna Gaines is "Hot Stuff"; what was her stage name?

Q309. What fabulously gifted singer/songwriter/producer wrote the music score of the 1972 film *Superfly*?

Q310. "Rock Your Baby" was a 1974 number 1 song for this Florida-born native, who was the husband of this Florida-born soul sister who had a 1975 number 1 song called "Rockin' Chair"; what are the names of this couple?

Q311. "Hope That We Can Be Together Soon," a powerful ballad performed by Harold Melvin and the Bluenotes, featured a female vocalist; who was she?

    a. Sharon Paige

    b. Minnie Riperton

    c. Jean Carn

    d. DeeDee Sharp

Q312. Which ten-member family group out of Memphis had a number 1 song in 1975—"Boogie Fever"?

    a. Tavares

    b. Sylvers

    c. Brick

    d. DeBarge

Q313. Sylvia Vanderpool Robinson had a number 1 R&B record in 1973 called "Pillow Talk;" she performed as part of what famous duo back in the fifties?

Q314. "Smiling Faces Sometimes (Tell Lies)"—so says which group?

    a. The Elgins

    b. The Temptations

    c. The O'Jays

    d. Undisputed Truth

*The encouragement of friend Bill Cosby gave Billy
Paul the push needed for his first public performance
at age eleven. A later meeting with Kenny Gamble
and Leon Huff led to his fame with "Me and Mrs.
Jones."*

Q315. The duo of Gene McFadden and John Whitehead
wrote and produced songs for many Philadelphia soul
acts—but in 1979 they produced and performed their
own number 1 R&B hit; what was the name of that
tune?

Q316. "She Works Hard for the Money" and she's one of the
"Bad Girls"; who is she?

Q317. Whose major 1976 hit was "Lowdown"?
　　　a. Stevie Wonder
　　　b. Boz Scaggs
　　　c. Ricky Skaggs
　　　d. Lionel Richie

Q318. Who was the former lead singer of the group whose
first major hit was "Machine Gun"?

Q319. Before which singing Pennyslvania-based sisters
struck out on their own, they were back-up for the
boss herself (Diana Ross)?

Q320. What group came together in Kansas City, Missouri,
but didn't enjoy success until their move to England
and the release of "Natural High"?

Q321. How do you spell the name of Ray Parker Jr.'s group?

Q322. Who was a member of the Jarmels and later the
Delfonics and had a solo hit with "Love Won't Let Me
Wait"?

    a. Wilbert Harrison
    b. Teddy Pendergrass
    c. Major Harris
    d. Freddie Jackson

Q323. Originally a writer, then a singer, what tall slender soul brother, collaborating with Brian Jackson, was rapping in the early seventies with "The Bottle" and "Johannesburg"?

Q324. Who stepped in as lead singer when Sam Cooke left the Soul Stirrers, and later everybody came to know him for songs such as "Cheaper To Keep Her" and "Jody's Got Your Girl and Gone"?
    a. Clyde McPhatter
    b. Wilson Pickett
    c. Johnnie Taylor
    d. Joe Tex

Q325. Who were featured artists on their only R&B number 1, "TSOP (The Sound of Philadelphia)"?
    a. Chapter 8
    b. Five Special
    c. Natural Four
    d. The Three Degrees

Q326. What group, named for three virtues and produced by Van McCoy, had a number 1 R&B hit in 1975 with "To Each His Own"?

Q327. Which lady of song has had an unparalleled career, but the height of her success on the R&B charts came in 1974 with "You're As Right As Rain"?

Q328. In 1974, whose plea was "Let's Straighten It Out"?
    a. Sylvester
    b. Z.Z. Hill
    c. Latimore
    d. Bobby Bland

Q329. With a career spanning more than thirty years, what group has had nineteen Top 10 records, including number 1 hits, "I'll Be Around" and "Mighty Love"?

Q330. What artist had a number 1 R&B hit back in 1973, another more recently in 1994 with several in between, and is known as the "Love Man"?

Q331. "Ring My Bell," a 1979 soul smash, was performed by which one-hit wonder?
   a. Meli'sa Morgan
   b. Shirley Murdoch
   c. Gloria Gaynor
   d. Anita Ward

Q332. What was Michael Jackson's first solo number 1 R&B hit?
   a. "Got To Be There"
   b. "Rock With You"
   c. "Ben"
   d. "Don't Stop 'Til You Get Enough"

Q333. After he lost four times at the Apollo amateur night, what singer would become a superstar for all time, to the surprise of the amateur-night audiences?
   a. James Brown
   b. Nat "King" Cole
   c. Michael Jackson
   d. Luther Vandross

Q334. Harmonica genius Lee Oskar was a part of what popular band, which until 1971 was rock star Eric Burdon's backup band?
   a. AWB
   b. Wild Cherry
   c. War
   d. Was (Not Was)

Q335. Lillian, Louise, and Carmen Lopez, three sisters from Connecticut, had a smash hit in 1977 called "Native New Yorker"; what was their group's name?
 a. Whistle
 b. Lace
 c. Odyssey
 d. Zhane

Q336. What group went to the top of the R&B charts with the 1976 smash "Who'd She Coo"?

Q337. "People all over the world join hands" and form what?

Q338. In 1978, the O'Jays made a record called "Brandy"; who was Brandy?
 a. wife
 b. girlfriend
 c. old friend
 d. pet dog

Q339. L.T.D., a fabulous soul band of the seventies, was fronted by which outstanding lead vocalist?
 a. Peabo Bryson
 b. Jeffrey Osborne
 c. J.T. Taylor
 d. Jimmy Castor

Q340. "Jack and Jill" was a major hit for this band and their talented founder/lead singer; what was the name of the group and the singer?

Q341. "Band of Gold," a 1970 monster hit from the production team of Holland-Dozier-Holland, was performed by what beautiful Detroit-born soul sister?

Q342. *Look Out for Number 1* was a platinum selling LP from which brother team known as "Thunderthumbs" and "Lightning Licks"?
 a. Tavares
 b. The Isley Brothers

    c. Brothers Johnson
    d. Cornelius Brothers

Q343. What band changed the sound of African-American music in the seventies by utilizing the sound of the *kalimba* (an African thumb piano)?

Q344. "Best of My Love" was a number 1 song in the late seventies from which family group out of Chicago?

Q345. Who composed the score for the 1972 movie *Trouble Man,* starring Robert Hooks?

Q346. Whose version of the Christmas favorite, "This Christmas" didn't hit the charts, but it's one of those songs we enjoy every year?

Q347. From 1973–1976 were stellar solo years for Eddie Kendricks—nine Top 10 R&B hits; which 1973 record was a number 1 pop *and* R&B hit?
    a. "Can I?"
    b. "Shoeshine Boy"
    c. "Keep On Truckin' (Part I)"
    d. "He's a Friend"

Q348. Who first came to prominence as a member of the Miles Davis Quintet in the sixties, and later formed the Headhunters and created the crossover hit "Chameleon"?

Q349. "Hey There Lonely Girl" came from what smooth singing soulful brother in 1970?
    a. Larry Graham
    b. Eddie Holman
    c. Freddie Scott
    d. Tyrone Davis

Q350. "Wanted young men single and free" is a line from the 1971 hit "Want Ads"; who sang this number 1 R&B hit?

In the late sixties, Sly and the Family Stone fused soul and psychedelic music into a new sound that captivated both white and black audiences. Before achieving stardom, Sly worked as a disc jockey at soul radio stations, KSOL and KDIA in San Francisco.

Q351. Their one big hit "Vehicle" sounded a lot like Blood, Sweat and Tears; who were they?

Q352. Which brother was rapping about the injustices of society back in the early seventies, when he hit the charts with "The Revolution Will Not Be Televised"?
   a. Sly Stone
   b. Frankie Beverly
   c. Curtis Mayfield
   d. Gil Scott-Heron

Q353. What popular Grammy–winning crooner was once managed by the late Sam Cooke, and created the annual telethon for the United Negro College Fund?

Q354. Who said "Be Thankful for What You Got"?
   a. Lenny Welch
   b. Al Green
   c. Andre Handy
   d. William DeVaughn

The Eighties and Nineties

The eighties and nineties have been full of R&B music diversity. Artists such as Luther Vandross, Prince, Anita Baker, New Edition, Lionel Richie, Whitney Houston, Boyz II Men, and, of course, the King of Pop, Michael Jackson, made a very positive mark on the entire world with their music.

Also, a new form of music took shape in the eighties and nineties known as rap. Led by early pioneers like the Sugarhill Gang, Kool Moe Dee, Run DMC, Chub Rock, Public Enemy, M.C. Hammer, and D. J. Jazzy Jeff and the Fresh Prince, rap music became a major force in the industry.

Female groups tasted success in a big way during the early nineties with EnVogue, SWV, and TLC kissing the top of the charts on several occasions. Janet Jackson, Mariah Carey, Mary J. Blige, and Brandy hit the big time as single performers.

Rhythm & Blues music has come a long way since the fifties and there's no reason to think that the popularity and success of soul music will let up anytime soon.

The Eighties and Nineties

Q355. Who is an Emmy-Award–winning choreographer/dancer/singer, wife of a former NBA star, and sister of a famous actress?

Q356. "Nite and Day" was the first of several R&B number 1 hits by what recording artist who was born Al Brown in Boston, Massachusetts and raised in Mt. Vernon, New York?

Q357. Who entered her "Rhythm of Life" in Yakima, Washington and was discovered by Tears for Fears?

Q358. What well-known author penned Marvin Gaye's hit, "Sexual Healing"? (Hint: He also wrote Marvin's biography *Divided Soul*.)
    a. Stephen King
    b. H. Steven Robinson
    c. David Ritz
    d. John Grisham

Q359. What is the name of the former school teacher with an enchanting falsetto who joined Kool and the Gang as lead singer?

Q360. What New Jersey–born and bred vocalist/model/actress is the daughter, the cousin, and the wife of well-known singers?

Q361. From 1986–1995, what well-known sister charted eleven number 1 R&B hits, while her superstar brother only had eight in the number-1 slot?

Q362. Eddie Kendricks, David Ruffin, Paul Williams, Melvin Franklin, and Otis Williams are most often remembered as the Temptations, but from 1961 through 1996 eleven other singers have been Temptations; what are the names of four of them?

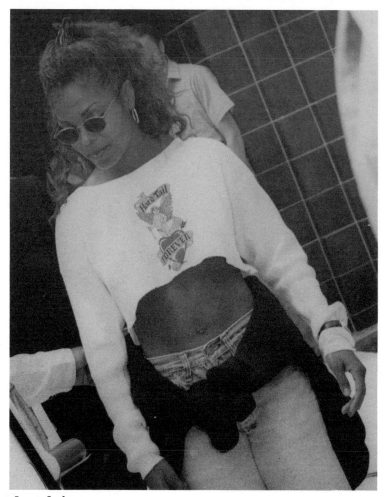

Janet Jackson

Q363. What famous rap duo made a 1991 cover of "Ring My Bell"?
    a. Public Enemy
    b. D.J. Jazzy Jeff and the Fresh Prince
    c. N.W.A.
    d. McFadden and Whitehead

The Fresh Prince a.k.a. Will Smith (left) and D. J. Jazzy Jeff a.k.a. Jeff Townes (left)

Q364. Who is the late singer/actress/fashion model who sang "If You Don't Wanna Change the World" and "Betcha By Golly, Wow"?

Q365. Eumir Deodato, a pop-jazz keyboardist, produced the number 1 hit "Celebration" for what group?

Q366. Who first sang gospel, next was a backup vocalist for Chaka Khan and Lou Rawls, and then had a modeling career—all before earning more than seven number 1 pop hits in the first eleven years of her recording career?

Q367. What former member of the Commodores became a superstar solo performer?

Q368. Whitney Houston's 1992 mega hit, "I Will Always Love You" was written and originally recorded by what major country star?
   a. Loretta Lynn
   b. Wynonna Judd
   c. Dolly Parton
   d. Reba McEntire

Q369. Peabo Bryson has won two Oscars for duets from soundtracks; what is the name of one of these award-winning songs?

Q370. L. A. Reid's cousin and Babyface's two brothers formed which group that had two number 1 hits in 1990?
   a. The Deele
   b. After 7
   c. The Dubs
   d. New Censation

Q371. What rap duo received a Grammy for the 1988 classic "Parents Just Don't Understand"?

Q372. What rap trio popularized hats, gold chains, and untied sneakers for their youthful audiences?
   a. Grandmaster Flash
   b. Run-D.M.C.
   c. Sugarhill Gang
   d. 2 Live Crew

New Yorker Gregory Abbot had a national number 1
hit with "Shake You Down" in 1986.

Kenneth "Babyface" Edmonds (left) and L. A. Reid institution (right), the two most successful record producers of the eighties and nineties

Q373. In 1987 who hit the big time with "Lean on Me," which was first recorded by Bill Withers in 1972?

Q374. What group had a number 1 R&B hit with "Word Up," featuring Larry Blackmon?

Q375. With a 1986 induction into the Rock and Roll Hall of Fame and a 1984 Grammy Lifetime Achievement Award, who is the original "Brown-Eyed Handsome Man"?

Q376. In 1984 Berry Gordy's son, Kennedy, had a big hit with "Somebody's Watching Me"; what name did he use?
   a. Rockwell
   b. Milli (of Milli Vanilli)
   c. Terence Trent D'Arby
   d. Prince

Q377. At the 1985 recording session for "We Are the World," who told each of the more than forty-five-plus arriving celebrities to "Leave your ego right there at the door"?
   a. Michael Jackson
   b. Bob Geldof
   c. Quincy Jones
   d. Lionel Richie

Q378. Whose stage image included long, cornrowed, and beaded hair, and as a producer created hits for Teena Marie and the Temptations?

Q379. In 1984 Ray Parker Jr. won a Grammy for best pop instrumental performance for what title tune from a movie?

Q380. Who was the lead singer for Harold Melvin and the Bluenotes before leaving to become a superstar solo performer?

Q381. In 1984 who won a Grammy for best female R&B vocal performance for "I Feel for You"?
   a. Marjorie Stewart
   b. Chaka Kahn
   c. Aretha Franklin
   d. Phyllis Hyman

Q382. In 1986 who joined with Dionne Warwick, Elton John, and Stevie Wonder on the Grammy-Award–winning, "That's What Friends Are For"?

Q383. What rap duo is known for a seven-inch-high vertical hairstyle, a clean-cut look, and achieved star status with their series of *House Party* movies?

Q384. What female band's "Meeting in the Ladies' Room" was one to be in on?

Q385. Which Obie-Award–winning actress/vocalist/dancer/ pianist gained national recognition with "Flash-dance...What a Feeling"?
   a. Irene Cara
   b. Angela Winbush
   c. Phoebe Snow
   d. Caira White

Q386. A great deal of controversy surrounded whose per-formance on C&C Music Factory's "Gonna Make You Sweat (Everybody Dance Now)"?
   a. Diana Ross
   b. Izora Rhodes
   c. Martha Wash
   d. Etta Jones

Q387. In 1982 who added to her list of hits with "Jump to It" (produced by Luther Vandross), and was declared a "natural resource" in 1985 by the state of Michigan?

Q388. Which vocalist of French-Cuban and Puerto Rican extraction was featured with Arthur Mitchell's Dance Theatre of Harlem, and about six years later had a hit with "Tonight I Give In"?
   a. Mariah Carey
   b. Angela Bofill
   c. Oleta Finch
   d. Sade

Q389. Everyone knows the Temptations sang "My Girl," but what groups recorded "When She Was My Girl" and "Used Ta Be My Girl"?
   a. The Chi-Lites and the Four Tops

b. The Four Tops and the O'Jays

c. The Chi-Lites and the Isley Brothers

d. The Contours and the O'Jays

Q390. What is the name of the group that inspired the 1991 movie *The Five Heartbeats*?

a. The Temptations

b. The Dells

c. Harold Melvin and the Bluenotes

d. The Chi-Lites

Q391. Which 1983 movie set off a revival of several Motown hits?

Q392. Whose choice of music over a football scholarship paid off when he was judged (by Quincy Jones) worthy of winning the 1987 Sony Innovator Talent Search?

a. Jeffrey Osborne

b. Jonathan Butler

c. Howard Hewett

d. Al B. Sure!

Q393. In 1988 which artist had a hit with "Wishing Well"?

a. Syreeta

b. Cuba Gooding

c. Terence Trent D'Arby

d. Lenny Kravitz

Q394. Before Dana Owens signed with Tommy Boy, acted on TV, or in the movies, she recorded with Troop and Levert, David Bowie, and Monie Love; by what name is she best known?

a. Grace Jones

b. Queen Latifah

c. Janet Jackson

d. M.C. Lyte

Q395. Which group sang "All This Love" and appeared to make it a family motto when three siblings went solo

and another two (not in the group named after the
family) were in Switch?
  a. The GAP Band
  b. DeBarge
  c. Tavares
  d. The Jackson 5

Q396. Even if you're not a fan of TV's *General Hospital,* you
may remember what smash hit by Patti Austin (with
James Ingram)?

Q397. It's "All the Way Live" on what group's "Fantastic
Voyage"?
  a. Lakeside
  b. The Olympics
  c. The Sensations
  d. The Wanderers

Q398. Who recorded Bob Dylan's "Emotionally Yours" and
came up with another in a long list of hits?

Q399. His dad's group scored in 1974 with "For the Love of
Money" and nearly fifteen years later which artist's
group followed suit with "Gotta Get the Money"?
  a. Cuba Gooding, Jr.
  b. Ziggy Marley
  c. Levi Stubbs, Jr.
  d. Gerald Levert

Q400. Who recorded "She's a Bad Mama Jama (She's Built,
She's Stacked)"?
  a. Stevie Wonder
  b. Junior
  c. Carl Carlton
  d. Joe Tex

Q401. What songstress topped the charts in 1990 with
"Vision of Love" and "Love Takes Time"?

Q402. The Commodores' "Nightshift" was a tribute to which two R&B giants?
  a. Eddie Kendricks and David Ruffin
  b. Marvin Gaye and Jackie Wilson
  c. Otis Redding and Marvin Gaye
  d. Johnny Ace and Otis Redding

Q403. The year was 1985 when which two Phils hit the charts together?
  a. Philip Bailey and Phil Collins
  b. Phillip Knight and Phil Collins
  c. Phil Flowers and Philip Bailey
  d. Philip Bailey and Phillip Knight

Q404. What were the names of their groups?

Q405. What was the name of their hit record?
  a. "Ebony and Ivory"
  b. "Walk This Way"
  c. "Easy Lover"
  d. "Say Say Say"

Q406. For singing "And I Am Telling You I'm Not Going" on Broadway and on record, who won a Tony and a Grammy?
  a. Jennifer Holliday
  b. Vanessa Williams
  c. Sheryl Lee Ralph
  d. Stephanie Mills

Q407. What group was asked by a record executive if they could make the grade, and they said, "Yes, We Can"?
  a. Sister Sledge
  b. The Jones Girls
  c. The Ronettes
  d. The Pointer Sisters

Q408. Who was accused of "perpetratin'" by his colleagues and responded with "U Can't Touch This"—the mega hit from his number 1 album that topped the charts for nearly half a year?
   a. M. C. Hammer
   b. Young MC
   c. Kurtis Blow
   d. Big Daddy Kane

Q409. Jodeci of "Lately" and "Come and Talk to Me" fame took their name from:
   a. Their desire to honor their hero, Joe Franklin from Washington, D.C.
   b. The name of a popular local DJ, 'Ice Doj.'
   c. Combining portions of three group members' stage names.
   d. None of the above.

Q410. What disco-era favorite sang "Pull Up to the Bumper"?
   a. Betty Davis
   b. Donna Summer
   c. Sylvester
   d. Grace Jones

Q411. Who recorded "Free Your Mind" and "My Lovin' (You're Never Gonna Get It)"?
   a. Tynea Handy & Her Crew
   b. TLC
   c. En Vogue
   d. Appolonia 6

Q412. Which raunchy soul sister toured with her own stage production, *Young Man, Older Woman*?
   a. Millie Jackson
   b. Moms Mabley
   c. Eartha Kitt
   d. Pearl Bailey

Q413. "Mama Used to Say" was a hit for what brother from England?

Q414. Who was the darling of the Broadway production, *The Wiz,* and had one of her biggest hits with "I Never Knew Love Like This Before"?
   a. Diana Ross
   b. Melba Moore
   c. Stephanie Mills
   d. Leslie Uggams

Q415. Who performed "Mama Said Knock You Out," a 1991 Grammy Award–winning rap single?
   a. Kool Moe Dee
   b. L.L. Cool "J"
   c. Big Daddy Kane
   d. M. C. Hammer

Q416. Which British soul trio had a string of hits including "Slow Down," "Don't Be a Fool," and "Hangin' on a String"?
   a. Atlantic Starr
   b. K.C. and the Sunshine Band
   c. Loose Ends
   d. Graham Central Station

Q417. Who is the Harlem-born sexy soul brother who hit the music scene with the 1987 number 1 smash "I Want Her"?
   a. Teddy Riley
   b. Keith Sweat
   c. Al B. Sure!
   d. Tevin Campbell

Q418. In 1984 what legendary lady won one of her many Grammys for the record of the year, "What's Love Got to Do With It"?

Tina Turner

Q419. Which West-Indies born soul brother came on strong with his 1984 million seller, "Caribbean Queen"?
a. Bob Marley
b. Billy Ocean
c. Jim Kelsey
d. Shabba Ranks

Q420. What trio was made up of two *Soul Train* dancers and a guy named Howard?

Q421. What are the names of the members of the group?
a. Howard Stern
b. Jeffrey Daniels
c. Howard Hewitt

    d. Chaka Khan

    e. Jody Watley

    f. Billy Preston

Q422. Dayton, Ohio, was the birthplace of which electro-funk band that introduced a fresh new sound to the soul music world with hits such as "Dance Floor" and "More Bounce to the Ounce"?

    a. Lillo Thomas

    b. Zapp (and Roger)

    c. Today

    d. R. J.'s Latest Arrival

Q423. What young rapper cowrote Tone Loc's "Wild Thing" and had a major hit of his own called "Bust a Move"?

    a. Mr. Lee

    b. Swamp Dog

    c. Luke

    d. Young MC

Q424. Shabba Ranks, a former DJ turned dancehall reggae singer, blasted onto the American music scene in the early nineties with which super hit?

    a. "Playaz Club"

    b. "Housecall (Your Body Can't Lie to Me)"

    c. "Do It to the Music"

    d. "All Time Lover"

Q425. What artist was a relative unknown with an unusual middle name who took "Thanks for My Child" to number 1 on the R&B charts in 1988?

Q426. Lionel Richie charted four number 1 singles in his solo career. Can you name them?

Q427. What gifted singer/producer and wife of soul legend Ronnie Isley was once half of a soul duo?

Q428. What was the name of the duo?

Q429. What forty-member choir had a major hit in 1991 called "Optimistic" which was produced by the award-winning team of Jimmy Jam and Terry Lewis?
- a. Edwin Hawkins Singers
- b. The Clara Ward Singers
- c. Sounds of Blackness
- d. Staple Singers

Q430. From 1979–1992, "The Artist Formerly Known as Prince" has had eight number 1 songs in his illustrious career. Can you name four of them?

Q431. What hip-hop foursome out of Jacksonville, Florida, had a 1994 smash entitled "Tootsee Roll"?
- a. Rude Boys
- b. 95 South
- c. Whodini
- d. 69 Boyz

Q432. "Call Me," "Start of a Romance," and "Real Love" were all number 1 songs for what self-contained soul band?
- a. War
- b. Commodores
- c. Skyy
- d. Mandrill

Q433. What 1983 album had the distinction of being the first to produce seven Top 10 hit singles?
- a. *Off the Wall*
- b. *Thriller*
- c. *Control*
- d. *Innervisions*

Q434. Their 1990 duet, "Where Do We Go From Here," earned which duo top position on the R&B charts?
- a. Janet Jackson and Luther Vandross
- b. Peaches and Herb
- c. Johnny Gill and Stacy Lattisaw
- d. Aretha Franklin and Levi Stubbs

Q435. "Remote Control" was a Top 5 hit for what group?
    a. LeVert
    b. The King Coles
    c. The Reddings
    d. The J. Robinsons

Q436. When the Temptations left Motown they signed on with what record label?
    a. Atlantic
    b. Sony
    c. Paisley Park
    d. United Artists

Q437. Roxie Roker (of *The Jeffersons*) was his mother, Lisa Bonet (of *The Cosby Show*) was his wife, and he had a hit with "It Ain't Over Til It's Over"; who is he?

Q438. What rap duo hit it big with "Jump" in 1995?

Q439. These two shared the same given name; what was it?

Q440. What were their "taken" names?

Q441. The Four Tops, formed in 1954, were inducted into the Rock and Roll Hall of Fame in 1989; as of 1997, how many Grammys have they been awarded?
    a. Five
    b. Two
    c. None
    d. One

Q442. "Ladies Love Cool James," but who is he?

Q443. The members of Bell Biv Devoe were originally in which group?
    a. New Birth
    b. New Edition
    c. New Censation
    d. New York City

Q444. Three brothers formed what soul group popular for such songs as "You Dropped a Bomb on Me" and "Early in the Morning"?

Q445. What "gentlemen of song" had the distinction of maintaining the same personnel for more than forty years?

Q446. Into the early nineties Motown continued to make a showing on the music charts with records such as "It's So Hard To Say Goodbye to Yesterday"; can you name the artist(s) who recorded it?

Q447. "Dial My Heart" was a hit for which group in 1988?
     a. DeBarge
     b. The Mad Lads
     c. The Boys
     d. De La Soul

Q448. Who is the soul group responsible for "Let It Whip"?
     a. Cameo
     b. The Dazz Band
     c. The Bar-Kays
     d. The Whispers

Q449. Kool (of Kool and the Gang) gets the award for bringing which group to the big time with their number 1 hit *All 4 Love*?
     a. Color Me Badd
     b. After 7
     c. Take 6
     d. Blackstreet

Q450. During his short but controversial life, what young rapper/actor created and performed several hits, including "Dear Mama" and "I Get Around"?

Q451. With seven number 1 R&B songs including "Never Too Much" and "Here and Now," what artist is a superstar?

Cameo, the classic soul funk band, was the brain-child of the Juilliard-School-of-Music-trained Larry Blackmon. They were originally known as the New York City Players until 1974 when they changed their name to Cameo.

Q452. "Closer Than Friends," "Shower Me With Your Love," and "You Are My Everything" were number 1 R&B songs from which New Jersey-based vocal trio?
   a. The Stylistics
   b. Surface
   b. The Dells
   d. The Moments

Q453. SWV is not only the name of this group of New York soul sisters, it also says what they are; what is the full name of this group?

Q454. "Hip Hop Hooray" was a number 1 R&B smash from what East Orange, New Jersey, trio?

Q455. Who is the first African-American woman to be crowned Miss America, and the first Miss America to have a number 1 R&B hit called "Dreamin'"?

Q456. Ernesto, Orlando, George, and Gregory Phillips, along with their cousin, lead singer Renee Diggs, formed which rocking sextet of the eighties?
   a. Klymaxx
   b. Starpoint
   c. Rare Earth
   d. B. T. Express

Q457. Which group was discovered by Gerald Levert and their first record "Mamacita" was a smash?
   a. Troop
   b. The Trammps
   c. TRIBE
   d. A Tribe Called Quest

Q458. What smooth singing soul crooner, who is also a member of New Edition, hit number 1 on the *Billboard* R&B charts in 1990 with his first solo effort?
   a. Bobby Brown
   b. Michael Bivins
   c. Ralph Tresvant
   d. Johnny Gill

Q459. What is the name of the record?
   a. "My My My"
   b. "Sensitivity"
   c. "If It Isn't Love"
   d. "Who's the Mack"

Q460. Which R&B funk trio from Oakland, California appeared in the movie *House Party 2,* and had five R&B number-1 hits in three years, including "Little Walter"?
   a. Gary Tom's Empire
   b. Tony! Toni! Toné!
   c. Timex Social Club
   d. Today

Q461. "Take Your Time (Do It Right)" was a number 1 song for which funk band in 1980?
   a. Mother's Finest
   b. Graham Central Station
   c. Atlantic Star
   d. S.O.S. Band

Q462. The record was originally called "The Electric Boogie," and from that record a dance craze was created—the Electric Slide; who sang "The Electric Boogie"?
   a. Minnie Riperton
   b. Laura Lee
   c. Damita Jo
   d. Marcia Griffiths

Q463. Born in Houston, raised in Harlem, which artist was truly a one-hit wonder with his 1986 number 1 song simply titled "The Rain"?
    a. Joe Jones
    b. Oran "Juice" Jones
    c. Jimmy Jones
    d. Johnny Jones

Q464. Which talented soul brother hails from Jacksonville, Florida, began his career at the tender age of eight, his hits include "Show Me" and "Here I Go Again"?
    a. Bobby Lewis
    b. Tony Payne
    c. Glenn Jones
    d. Jay Johnson

Q465. The sons of the O'Jays' lead singer have a group of their own; what is the name of the group?

Q466. What is Stanley Kirk Burrell also known as?
    a. M.C. Bleed
    b. M.C. Shy D
    c. Slick Rick
    d. M.C. Hammer

Q467. M.C. Hammer used the music track from Rick James's "Super Freak" to create his biggest song ever; what was it?

Q468. They were first known as the Butlers, then Raw Soul, finally they became Maze; what is the name of their lead singer?

Q469. Which Brooklyn-raised female rapper's biggest hit to date is a rap classic titled "Ruffneck"?
    a. M. C. Ren
    b. M. C. Lyte
    c. Queen Latifah
    d. Patra

Q470. Dionne Warwick teamed up with three other super-stars in 1985 to record "That's What Friends Are For"; what were the names of the other artists?

Q471. "Just the Two of Us" was a hit for Grover Washington, Jr., the world-renowned saxophonist, and which male who provided vocal accompaniment?
   a. George Benson
   b. Johnny Mathis
   c. Bill Withers
   d. Freddie Jackson

Q472. What family gospel quartet consists of brothers Michael, Ronald, and twins Marvin and Carvin?

Q473. The 1993 number 1 ballad "Knockin' Da Boots" was made by what group?
   a. H-Town
   b. The Boys
   c. Hi-Five
   d. Whodini

Q474. "I'll Take You There" has been a number 1 song twice, once in 1972 with Mavis Staples singing lead with the Staple Singers, then again in 1991 with Mavis accompanying what artists?

Q475. The Stone City Band was the backup band for which popular rock and R&B performer?

Q476. Rita Wright, a Pittsburgh soul sister who was once married to Stevie Wonder, used what stage name?

Q477. Who started her career, at age seven, on *The Cosby Show,* and also recorded the mildly successful "That's What Little Girls Are For"?
   a. Brandy
   b. Stacy Lattisaw
   c. Jasmine Guy
   d. Raven Symone

> *Early in his career, Freddie Jackson worked as a word processor by day and a backup vocalist for Evelyn "Champagne" King and Angela Bofill, among others, at night.*

Q478. Martha Wash and Izora Rhodes were backup singers for Sylvester and they also recorded under the name Two Tons O'Fun. Later they changed their name to which of the following?
  a. First Choice
  b. The Weather Girls
  c. The Ravens
  d. Xscape

Q479. Robert Van Winkle, a blue-eyed rapper from Miami, is best known by which name?
  a. Kris Kross
  b. Method Man
  c. Vanilla Ice
  d. Junior

Q480. In 1984, Dennis Edwards (a many-time member of the Temptations) had a solo hit featuring vocalist Siedah Garrett; what was that hit?

Q481. What are Bebe and Cece Winans' given names?
  a. Robert and Cecilia
  b. Benjamin and Priscilla
  c. Ronald and Crista
  d. William and Coretta

Q482. Which talented vocalist/keyboardist enjoyed success as a member of the Doobie Brothers, but really hit it big when he teamed up with Patti Labelle on the 1986 number 1 hit "On My Own"?
  a. Peabo Bryson
  b. George Michael
  c. Daryl Hall
  d. Michael McDonald

Q483. What Cleveland, Ohio, duo of David Tolliver and Jason Champ weighed over 300 pounds each and were discovered by Gerald Levert?
   a. The Fat Boys
   b. Men at Large
   c. Soul II Soul
   d. The Overweight Lovers

Q484. Who became a superstar as a solo performer, but achieved his first success with a group called Wham!?
   a. James Ingram
   b. George Michael
   c. Donny Hathaway
   d. Billy Preston

Q485. "Shake Your Thang" and "Shoop" are hit songs by which Queens, New York–based female rap trio?
   a. M.C. Lyte
   b. TLC
   c. SWV
   d. Salt-n-Pepa

Q486. What Nigerian-born sexy female soul singer hit the American scene in a large way in 1984 with the hit single "Hang On to Your Love"?

Singer, songwriter, and keyboardist Donny Hathaway was best known for his duets with Roberta Flack. His biggest hit, recorded with Flack in 1978, was a gold single, "The Closer I Get To You." Hathaway died in January 1979 after falling out of his fifteenth-floor room window in New York City's Essex House Hotel. Police called it suicide; close friends said no way.

Q487. Who was the female superstar who accompanied Lionel Richie on his 1981 number 1 song?

Q488. What is the name of the record?

Q489. This mega-talented soul brother formed his own trio in 1988 and took the music world by storm with such hits as "Groove Me," "I Like," and "Let's Chill"; what is the name of the artist and the group?

Q490. Producer/DJ Pete Rock works with which rapper from Mt. Vernon, New York?
  a. Kool Moe Dee
  b. C.L. Smooth
  c. Eazy E
  d. Kurtis Blow

Q491. Blackstreet soared high on the charts with "Before I Let You Go"; what is the name of their lead singer, a well-known New Jack Swing producer and former member of Guy?
  a. L. A. Reid
  b. Carlin O. Stewart Jr.
  c. Teddy Riley
  d. Jimmy Jam

Q492. Some know her as a Nancy Wilson protégé, some know her as NBA star John Battle's wife, and others know her as a fantastic singer; who is she?

Q493. A graduate of Washington, D.C.'s Duke Ellington School of the Arts, which smooth young artist gained national recognition from "With You"?
  a. Aaron Hall
  b. Aaron Neville
  b. Chris Jasper
  d. Tony Terry

Q494. "Living in America," from the film *Rocky IV,* was one of whose chart busters?

Diana Ross

Q495. Most of his hits have been collaborations with other singers, but in 1990 who had a solo number 1 with "I Don't Have the Heart"?

Q496. "A Little Bit More" was a 1986 number 1 R&B hit for which twosome?
   a. James Ingram and Patti Austin
   b. Melba Moore and Freddie Jackson
   c. BeBe and CeCe Winans
   d. Diana Ross and Lionel Richie

Q497. Which one of these groups recorded for Motown in 1988 and had a Top 20 hit with "Tired of Being Alone"?
   a. Choice Four
   b. First Choice
   c. The Right Choice
   d. New Choice

Q498. These gentlemen formed what à capella group (originally called Alliance) and are classified as gospel, jazz-oriented, etc., which didn't stop their R&B success with the 1990 Grammy-winning album *So Much 2 Say*?

Q499. Guy was the name of the group, and Teddy Riley was their founder; what are the names of the other two members who were siblings?
    a. James and Bobby Purify
    b. Gerald and Sean Levert
    c. Percy and Curtis Mayfield
    d. Aaron and Damion Hall

Q500. "Juicy Fruit" went to the top of the R&B charts for what group named for their leader?

Q501. Between 1992 and 1994 which lovely talented Maryland-born lady had six records in the Top 20?
    a. Tisha (Campbell)
    b. Shirley Jones
    c. Renee Diggs
    d. Toni Braxton

Q502. Who, by the time he reached the tender age of sixteen, had four number 1 hits to his credit, including "Can We Talk"?

Q503. Who said, "And the Beat Goes On," then they told us to "Rock Steady"?

Q504. What singer/actress had four Top 5 R&B hits, including "Sittin' Up in My Room" (Featuring L.L. Cool J)?
    a. Monifa
    b. Sybil
    c. Brandy
    d. Lori K.

Q505. "Lean on Me" was a R&B hit in the Top 5 for what singer in 1972, and for what group in 1986?

Q506. Stevie Wonder produced and arranged the hit "Let's Get Serious" for what Motown performer?

Q507. Which Marvin Gaye record stayed number 1 on the R&B charts the longest?
  a. "Sexual Healing"
  b. "I Heard It Through the Grapevine"
  c. "You're All I Need to Get By"
  d. "Let's Get It On"

Q508. In 1987 this dancer/actor/singer shared a number 1 R&B hit with Luther Vandross; what is the name of the singer and the song?

Q509. Who was discovered by "The Artist Formerly Known as Prince," and costarred with his royal badness in *Purple Rain*?
  a. Vanity
  b. Appollonia
  c. Sheila E.
  d. Vesta

Q510. Who co-hosted TV's *Solid Gold* in the eighties and has been a major star since the sixties with hits such as "Don't Make Me Over" and "Anyone Who Had a Heart"?

Q511. Leslie Sebastian Charles was the male vocalist on the 1988 number 1 hit "Get Outta My Dreams, Get Into My Car"; what is his stage name?
  a. Major Harris
  b. Billy Ocean
  c. Major Lance
  d. Chuck Cissel

Q512. N.W.A., a very successful rap group of the early nineties, produced three solo artists from their original four-man crew. Their given names were: Eric Wright, Andre Young, and O'Shea Jackson; what were their stage names?

Q513. Who is the only NBA all-star to have a Top 20 rap record?

Q514. Which foxy lady paid her soul dues as a backup singer for Melba Moore, Whitney Houston, Kashif, and Chaka Khan before hitting the R&B number 1 spot with "Do Me Baby"?
   a. Meli'sa Morgan
   b. Mariah Carey
   c. Donna Washington
   d. Flavia Payne

Q515. Which very funny man teamed up with Rick James in 1985 to "Party All the Time"?
   a. Sinbad
   b. Richard Pryor
   c. Eddie Murphy
   d. Will Smith

Q516. Who was a former backup singer for Zapp and had her debut solo album produced by funk great Roger Troutman?
   a. Millie Jackson
   b. Betty Wright
   c. Randy Crawford
   d. Shirley Murdoch

Cissy Houston (Whitney's mom), along with Dee Dee and Dionne Warwick, and Judy and Sylvia Guions, were the original members of The Sweet Inspirations gospel group. Dee Dee, Dionne, and Judy left the group, leaving Cissy and Sylvia with two new members to back up such stars as Neil Diamond, Dusty Springfield, Wilson Pickett, and Elvis Presley.

Q517. Who is a very talented New York-born saxophonist and his biggest hit was "I'll Be Good to You" featuring Vesta Williams?
   a. George Howard
   b. Najee
   c. Grover Washington
   d. Kim Waters

Q518. Naughty By Nature, the rap trio from New Jersey, had a 1991 hit, "O.P.P."; what did O.P.P. stand for?

Q519. What are the names of the five original members of the Boston-based superstars New Edition?

Q520. In 1986, Bobby Brown left New Edition to pursue a solo career; who was his replacement?

Q521. Who were the 1993 Grammy Award winners for best rap performance by a duo or group for the song "Rebirth of Slick (Cool Like Dat)"?

Q522. Who is the foxy lady who choreographed videos for several artists and became a star herself when she recorded the double platinum album *Forever Your Girl* in 1988?

Q523. "Diamonds" was a major smash for which guy, who used the Jimmy Jam–Terry Lewis production team and superstar Janet Jackson to hit the top of the R&B charts in 1987?

East Orange, New Jersey rap trio, Naughty By Nature was discovered by Queen Latifah. Their first release, "O.P.P." sold more than two million copies.

Early rappers Eric B and Rakim were sued by the legendary Godfather of Soul, James Brown, when they used fragments (samples) of his music on their records. The suit was settled out of court.

Q524. "The Show" was a classic rap hit from what very talented organization?

Q525. On "Two Occasions" between 1983 and 1988, what Cincinnati-based group had Top 10 hits?
    a. The Time
    b. The Deele
    c. The Parliament
    d. De La Soul

Q526. What producer/songwriter/singer came from this group?

Q527. What versatile superstar performer has won eight gospel Grammy Awards, and in 1994 recorded a duet with country star Lyle Lovett to win a ninth Grammy?

Q528. This artist was, and is, a major star in the rap world; his given name is Dwight Myers; what is his stage name?

Q529. Who became rap music's most controversial artist in 1992 with his "Cop Killer"?

Q530. Singer Melba Moore gave what vocalist the exposure he needed to eventually obtain star status?

Q531. In 1990, a number 1 R&B hit called "Where Do We Go From Here" was recorded by which two childhood friends?

Q532. Who started as fraternity brothers on the campus of Howard University, and in 1992 hit the big time with "If I Ever Fall in Love"?
   a. Pure Soul
   b. Shai
   c. II D Extreme
   d. Immature

Q533. We were caught up in the *Rapture* with whose "Sweet Love"?

Answers

The Fifties and Sixties

A1. Etta James and Harvey Fuqua

A2. a. Patti LaBelle

A3. a. Johnny Carter

A4. Tammi Terrell

A5. d. Marvin Gaye

A6. c. Chuck Barksdale

A7. Jimi Hendrix (a.k.a. Jimmy James)

A8. a. Maurice White

A9. Diana Ross, Mary Wilson, Florence Ballard

A10. c. Little Anthony and the Imperials

A11. Patti LaBelle and the Blue Belles

A12. b. Johnny Carter (of the Dells)

A13. Archie Bell and the Drells

A14. b. Hank Ballard (of Hank Ballard and the Midnighters)

A15. Diana Ross, Tammi Terrell, Mary Wells, and Kim Weston

A16. Marvin Gaye

A17. c. Bobby Taylor (of Bobby Taylor and the Vancouvers)

A18. b. "I Heard It Through the Grapevine"

A19. Billy Stewart

A20. Berry Gordy

A21. a. The Vibrations

A22. c. The Crystals

A23. James Brown

A24. b. Arthur Conley

A25. Solomon Burke, Arthur Conley, Don Covay, Ben E. King, Wilson Pickett, and Joe Tex

A26. The Contours

A27. a. Ruth Brown

A28. a. Clyde McPhatter

A29. c. Fats Domino

A30. Sonny Til and the Orioles

A31. Jimi Hendrix

A32. c. "Try Me"

A33. d. T-Neck

A34. Little Richard

A35. Booker T and the MGs

A36. The Originals

A37. a. Joe Cuba Sextet

A38. Don Covay and Aretha Franklin

A39. Levi Stubbs, Renaldo "Obie" Benson, Abdul "Duke" Fakir, and Lawrence Payton

A40. Jerry Butler

A41. Gordy, Motown, Soul, Tamla, VIP

A42. c. Hitsville, U.S.A. (Motown)

A43. b. Shorty Long

A44. Etta James

A45. c. Frankie Lymon

A46. d. Ernie K-Doe

A47. The Platters

A48. James and Bobby Purify

A49. c. "Why Do Fools Fall in Love"

A50. d. Chris Kenner

A51. B. B. King

A52. b. Bobby Day

A53. c. The Bobbettes

A54. b. Friends of Distinction

A55. a. Chuck Jackson

A56. c. *Dirty Dancing*

A57. c. Maurice Williams and the Zodiacs

A58. c. The Uptown

A59. b. Screamin' Jay Hawkins

A60. c. The Shirelles

A61. The Toys

A62. c. The Chantels

A63. b. Gene Chandler

A64. "Heat Wave," 1963; "Dancing in the Street," 1964; Martha and the Vandellas

A65. Della Reese

A66. Ruby and the Romantics

A67. d. Little Willie John

A68. d. The Five Satins

A69. b. Betty Everett

A70. d. The Spaniels

A71. a. Cindy Birdsong

A72. c. Valerie Simpson

A73. b. Joe Tex

A74. "Tossin' and Turnin'"

A75. The Ramsey Lewis Trio

A76. Little Richard

A77. b. Tammi Terrell

A78. d. Marvin Gaye

A79. b. Carla Thomas

A80. James Brown

A81. c. Sam and Dave

A82. b. The Jackson 5

A83. c. "I Want You Back"

A84. d. Shep and the Limelites

A85. d. Joe Simon

A86. The Shirelles

A87. b. "Let the Good Times Roll"

A88. Sam Moore and Dave Prater

A89. d. Robert Parker

A90. The (Young) Rascals

A91. a. Lou Rawls

A92. b. Sir Mack Rice

A93. c. The Righteous Brothers

A94. Otis Redding

A95. b. Bar-Kays

A96. b. Eugene Record

A97. The Chi-Lites

A98. The Raeletts (Ray Charles)

A99. d. The Radiants

A100. The Spaniels

A101. b. Lloyd Price

A102. c. Procol Harum

A103. b. Young-Holt Unlimited

A104. c. Percy Sledge

A105. b. "Since I Don't Have You"

A106. b. The Flamingos

A107. b. Brenda Holloway

A108. c. The Tams

A109. Johnny Mathis

A110. "Stagger Lee"

A111. Ben E. King

A112. The Drifters

A113. Jimmy Ruffin

A114. b. "I Can't Get Next to You"

A115. b. Cholly Atkins

A116. Barrett Strong

A117. c. The Tymes

A118. b. Little Willie John

A119. a. Marvin Gaye

A120. c. The Coasters

A121. The Clovers

A122. a. The Teen Queens

A123. d. Jesse Belvin

A124. d. Dobie Gray

A125. Bobby Freeman

A126. Marvin Gaye and Kim Weston

A127. b. The Elgins

A128. c. Larry Williams

A129. William "Smokey" Robinson

A130. Florence Ballard

A131. "My Girl"

A132. b. The Unifics

A133. a. "Happy, Happy Birthday Baby"

A134. d. Peaches and Herb

A135. d. The Stylistics

A136. d. Bettye Swann

A137. b. Sweet Inspirations

A138. a. Chuck Willis

A139. The Turbans

A140. The Soul Children

A141. d. Linda Jones

A142. Jerry Butler and Curtis Mayfield

A143. Billy Davis and Marilyn McCoo

A144. Dionne Warwick (Sister: Dee Dee; Aunt: Cissy Houston)

A145. b. Dinah Washington

A146. Baby Washington

A147. b. Johnny Otis

A148. c. Jackie Wilson

A149. d. The Winstons

A150. b. Gene McDaniels

A151. "Treasure of Love," "Long Lonely Nights," and "A Lover's Question"

A152. b. Mel and Tim

A153. d. The Meters

A154. "Hold On I'm Coming" and "Soul Man"

A155. b. Sam the Sham and the Pharaohs

A156. Bobby Womack

A157. c. Minnie Riperton

A158. Smokey Robinson

A159. James Brown (Soul Brother Number One)

A160. Mary Wells

A161. a. The Jarmels

A162. Aretha Franklin

A163. b. Lesley Gore

A164. d. "Shop Around"

A165. a. Willie Bobo

A166. The Schoolboys

A167. "Please Mr. Postman"

A168. c. Barry White

A169. O.C. Smith

A170. Hugh Masekela, "Grazing in the Grass"

A171. Miriam Makeba, "Pata Pata"

A172. "Get Ready," "Ain't Too Proud To Beg," "Beauty Is Only Skin Deep," and "(I Know) I'm Losing You"

A173. d. The Vontastics

A174. Jr. Walker and the All Stars

A175. b. The Del-Vikings

A176. b. The O'Kaysions

A177. Aaron Neville

A178. c. Bobby Rodgers

A179. d. Jr. Walker

A180. Bobby Darin

A181. d. The Penguins

A182. b. "In the Midnight Hour"

A183. c. Faye Adams

A184. Bo Diddley

A185. Fats Domino

A186. b. The Dixie Cups

A187. d. Bill Doggett

A188. c. Lee Dorsey

A189. d. Shirley Ellis

A190. The 5th Dimension

A191. a. The "5" Royales

A192. Ray Bryant; Dee Dee Sharp; and, Rufus Thomas

A193. Diana Ross and the Supremes had one R&B number 1 hit; the Supremes had seven

A194. b. The Edwin Hawkins Singers

A195. David Ruffin

A196. b. Joe Turner

A197. Roy Hamilton

A198. b. Slim Harpo

A199. c. Wilbert Harrison

A200. Four

A201. Isaac Hayes

A202. "Sunny"

A203. c. Jesse Hill

A204. Billie Holiday

A205. Otis Redding

A206. Dinah Washington

A207. d. The Artistics

A208. "Little Esther" Phillips

A209. The Exciters

The Seventies

A210. a. 1977

A211. The Beginning of the End

A212. Bobby Womack

A213. a. Rick James

A214. Peaches and Herb

A215. James Brown

A216. c. Merry Clayton

A217. b. Con Funk Shun

A218. The Commodores

A219. a. The Hues Corporation

A220. a. Ruth Brown

A221. Stevie Wonder

A222. Jimmy Castor (Jimmy Castor Bunch)

A223. (Nick) Ashford and (Valerie) Simpson

A224. The Blackbyrds

A225. a. B. T. Express

A226. Billy Paul

A227. a. King Floyd

A228. d. Evelyn "Champagne" King

A229. a. Chaka Khan

A230. K. C. and the Sunshine Band

A231. Chic

A232. Eddie Kendricks

A233. Three Dog Night

A234. The Jets; the Five Stairsteps and Cubie; DeBarge; and Tavares

A235. Aretha Franklin, James Brown, Bob Marley (and You)

A236. b. Blue Magic

A237. Brook Benton; Gladys Knight and the Pips; and Ray Charles

A238. c. Tyrone Davis

A239. Roberta Flack

A240. c. Billy Preston

A241. b. Isaac Hayes

A242. *Shaft*

A243. d. Van McCoy

A244. b. The Bee Gees

A245. Minnie Riperton

A246. b. Chairmen of the Board

A247. The Temptations, Ron Banks and the Dramatics, Love Unlimited, and Dee Clark

A248. c. Dorothy Moore

A249. c. The Delfonics

A250. d. Tavares

A251. a. Lionel Richie

A252. Natalie Cole

A253. b. The Supremes

A254. a. Johnny Nash

A255. Commodores, the Isley Brothers, and Lou Rawls

A256. c. Carl Douglas

A257. The Four Tops

A258. b. William Bell

A259. George Benson

A260. d. LaBelle

A261. The Main Ingredient

A262. The Manhattans

A263. c. Sly (of the Family Stone)

A264. The Stylistics

A265. c. Sugarhill Gang

A266. c. Johnnie Taylor

A267. c. Joe Tex

A268. a. "Proud Mary"

A269. b. War

A270. b. Ohio Players

A271. The O'Jays

A272. c. The Chi-Lites

A273. George Clinton (Parliament/Funkadelic)

A274. c. Wonderlove

A275. c. Ohio Players

A276. d. Billy Preston

A277. c. Sister Sledge

A278. b. The Cornelius Brothers and Sister Rose

A279. Smokey Robinson and the Miracles (Birthdate of Smokey Robinson and Bobby Rogers)

A280. b. Mary Jane

A281. *Innervisions* (1973) or *Fulfillingness' First Finale* (1974)

A282. Al Green

A283. a. Gloria Gaynor

A284. Hot Chocolate

A285. Penny (Nickname for Millicent)

A286. Donny Hathaway

A287. Roberta Flack

A288. c. The Fuzz

A289. "Quiet Storm"

A290. The Brothers Johnson

A291. Luther Ingram

A292. b. Billy Paul

A293. Donna Summer

A294. c. Mary Wilson

A295. d. Edwin Starr

A296. b. Switch

A297. "I Can See Clearly Now"

A298. "Show and Tell"

A299. c. Candi Staton

A300. The Staple Singers

A301. "I'll Take You There" and "Let's Do It Again"

A302. b. Stargard

A303. c. The Supremes

A304. c. James Taylor

A305. b. The Trammps

A306. a. Billy Griffin

A307. c. Honey Cone

A308. Donna Summer

A309. Curtis Mayfield

A310. George and Gwen McCrae

A311. a. Sharon Paige

A312. b. Sylvers

A313. Sylvia (of Mickey and Sylvia)

A314. d. Undisputed Truth

A315. "Ain't No Stopping Us Now"

A316. Donna Summer

A317. b. Boz Scaggs

A318. Lionel Richie (formerly of the Commodores)

A319. The Jones Girls

A320. Bloodstone

A321. R-a-y-d-i-o

A322. c. Major Harris

A323. Gil Scott-Heron

A324. c. Johnnie Taylor

A325. d. The Three Degrees

A326. Faith, Hope, and Charity

A327. Nancy Wilson

A328. c. Latimore

A329. The Spinners

A330. Barry White

A331. d. Anita Ward

A332. d. "Don't Stop 'Til You Get Enough"

A333. d. Luther Vandross

A334. c. War

A335. c. Odyssey

A336. The Ohio Players

A337. A "Love Train" (O'Jays)

A338. d. pet dog

A339. b. Jeffrey Osborne

A340. Raydio and Ray Parker, Jr.

A341. Freda Payne

A342. c. Brothers Johnson

A343. Earth, Wind and Fire

A344. The Emotions

A345. Marvin Gaye

A346. Donny Hathaway

A347. c. "Keep On Truckin' (Part I)"

A348. Herbie Hancock

A349. b. Eddie Holman

A350. Honey Cone

A351. Ides of March

A352. d. Gil Scott-Heron

A353. Lou Rawls

A354. d. William DeVaughn

The Eighties and Nineties

A355. Debbi Allen

A356. Al B. Sure!

A357. Oleta Adams

A358. c. David Ritz

A359. James "J.T." Taylor

A360. Whitney Houston

A361. Janet Jackson and Michael Jackson

A362. Elbridge (Al) Bryant, Dennis Edwards, Richard Street, Ricky Owens, Damon Harris, Glenn Leonard, Louis Price, Ron Tyson, Ali Ollie Woodson, Theo Peoples, and Ray Davis

A363. b. D.J. Jazzy Jeff and the Fresh Prince

A364. Phyllis Hyman

A365. Kool and the Gang

A366. Whitney Houston

A367. Lionel Richie

A368. c. Dolly Parton

A369. "A Whole New World (Aladdin's Theme)" or "Beauty and the Beast"

A370. b. After 7

A371. D.J. Jazzy Jeff and the Fresh Prince

A372. b. Run-D.M.C.

A373. Club Nouveau

A374. Cameo

A375. Chuck Berry

A376. a. Rockwell

A377. c. Quincy Jones

A378. Rick James

A379. "Ghostbusters"

A380. Teddy Pendergrass

A381. b. Chaka Kahn

A382. Gladys Knight

A383. Kid 'n' Play

A384. Klymaxx

A385. a. Irene Cara

A386. c. Martha Wash

A387. Aretha Franklin

A388. b. Angela Bofill

A389. b. The Four Tops and the O'Jays

A390. b. The Dells

A391. *The Big Chill*

A392. d. Al B. Sure!

A393. c. Terence Trent D'Arby

A394. b. Queen Latifah

A395. b. DeBarge

A396. "Baby, Come to Me"

A397. a. Lakeside

A398. The O'Jays

A399. d. Gerald Levert

A400. c. Carl Carlton

A401. Mariah Carey

A402. b. Marvin Gaye and Jackie Wilson

A403. a. Philip Bailey and Phil Collins

A404. Earth, Wind and Fire and Genesis

A405. c. "Easy Lover"

A406. a. Jennifer Holliday

A407. d. The Pointer Sisters

A408. a. M. C. Hammer

A409. c. Combining portions of 3 group members' stage names.

A410. d. Grace Jones

A411. c. En Vogue

A412. a. Millie Jackson

A413. Junior

A414. c. Stephanie Mills

A415. b. L.L. Cool "J"

A416. c. Loose Ends

A417. b. Keith Sweat

A418. Tina Turner

A419. b. Billy Ocean

A420. Shalamar

A421. b. Jeffrey Daniels; e. Jody Watley; and c. Howard Hewitt

A422. b. Zapp (and Roger)

A423. d. Young MC

A424. b. "Housecall (Your Body Can't Lie to Me)"

A425. Cheryl "Pepsii" Riley

A426. "All Night Long," "Hello," "Say You, Say Me," and "Do It to Me"

A427. Angela Winbush

A428. René and Angela

A429. c. Sounds of Blackness

A430. a. "I Wanna Be Your Lover," "When Doves Cry," "Let's Go Crazy," "Kiss," "Sign 'o' The Times," "Bat Dance," "Thieves in the Temple," "Diamonds and Pearls"

A431. d. 69 Boyz

A432. c. Skyy

A433. b. *Thriller*

A434. c. Johnny Gill and Stacy Lattisaw

A435. c. The Reddings

A436. a. Atlantic

A437. Lenny Kravitz

A438. Kris Kross

A439. Chris

A440. Mack Daddy and Daddy Mack

A441. c. None

A442. L. L. Cool J.

A443. b. New Edition

A444. The Gap Band

A445. The Four Tops

A446. Boyz II Men

A447. c. The Boys

A448. b. The Dazz Band

A449. c. Take 6

A450. Tupac Shakur

A451. Luther Vandross

A452. b. Surface

A453. Sisters With Voices

A454. Naughty By Nature

A455. Vanessa Williams

A456. b. Starpoint

A457. a. Troop

A458. c. Ralph Tresvant

A459. b. "Sensitivity"

A460. b. Tony! Toni! Toné!

A461. d. S.O.S. Band

A462. d. Marcia Griffiths

A463. b. Oran "Juice" Jones

A464. c. Glenn Jones

A465. Levert (their father is Eddie Levert)

A466. d. M.C. Hammer

A467. "U Can't Touch This"

A468. Frankie Beverly

A469. b. M.C. Lyte

A470. Gladys Knight, Stevie Wonder and Elton John

A471. c. Bill Withers

A472. The Winans

A473. a. H-Town

A474. BeBe and CeCe Winans

A475. Rick James

A476. Syreeta

A477. d. Raven Symone

A478. b. The Weather Girls

A479. c. Vanilla Ice

A480. "Don't Look Any Further"

A481. b. Benjamin and Priscilla

A482. d. Michael McDonald

A483. b. Men at Large

A484. b. George Michael

A485. d. Salt-n-Pepa

A486. Sade

A487. Diana Ross

A488. "Endless Love"

A489. Teddy Riley; Guy

A490. b. C. L. Smooth

A491. c. Teddy Riley

A492. Regina Belle

A493. d. Tony Terry

A494. James Brown

A495. James Ingram

A496. b. Melba Moore and Freddie Jackson

A497. c. The Right Choice

A498. Take 6

A499. d. Aaron and Damion Hall

A500. Mtume

A501. d. Toni Braxton

A502. Tevin Campbell

A503. The Whispers

A504. c. Brandy

A505. Bill Withers and Club Nouveau

A506. Jermaine Jackson

A507. a. "Sexual Healing" (10 weeks)

A508. Gregory Hines, "There's Nothing Better Than Love"

A509. b. Appollonia

A510. Dionne Warwick

A511. b. Billy Ocean

A512. Eazy-E, Dr. Dre, and Ice Cube

A513. Shaquille O'Neal

A514. a. Meli'sa Morgan

A515. c. Eddie Murphy

A516. d. Shirley Murdoch

A517. b. Najee

A518. Other People's Property

A519. Bobby Brown, Michael Bivins, Ricky Bell, Ronnie DeVoe and Ralph Tresvant

A520. Johnny Gill

A521. Digable Planets

A522. Paula Abdul

A523. Herb Alpert

A524. Doug E Fresh and the Get Fresh Crew

A525. b. The Deele

A526. Kenneth (Babyface) Edmonds

A527. Al Green

A528. Heavy D

A529. Ice T

A530. Freddie Jackson

A531. Stacy Lattisaw and Johnny Gill

A532. b. Shai

A533. Anita Baker